REDHEAD
IN THE CLOUDS

How I started Headcorn Aerodrome

The colourful life of
Diana Patten

As told to Greer Harris

First published in 2014 by Berforts Ltd

A catalogue record of this book is available from
The British Library

ISBN 978-1-908616-76-0

Typesetting in Garamond Pro and
book design by Eddie Sturgeon, Berforts Ltd

Printed in Great Britain by
Berforts Ltd, Hastings

Foreword

My mother was born into a world of wealth and high society and the last legacy of the Victorian era. She was taught right from wrong at an early age and I think this is what made her a bit of a rebel, 'always pushing the boundaries'.

She grew up not wanting for much but unfortunately those days were not to last. However her natural *jeux de vie* was a great help and was never behind the drag curve but in front at all times and at whatever cost!

You will read from her exploits that she had little fear. She is also caring and considerate and has a knack of disarming difficult situations with a flourish. She is very much a 'people person' and has always known how to put an event together that would be, fun and enjoyable and talked about for months afterwards!

Diana was never out of place wherever she was and certainly would not let the side down. As for being the centre of attention, yes, she was a lot of the time and did not mind that either! Flying was in her blood from an early age with her Aunt Paddy Naismith as a role model and this presented another exciting challenge that Diana took up with her usual verve.

Without that unique spirit, strength of character and innate charm I don't think Diana could have achieved the remarkable amount that she has done. Many people, including me, certainly have reason to be grateful for her inspiration.

Jamie Freeman
Headcorn Aerodrome

Silver Spoons

I watched, enthralled, as the small, red and white plane soared towards the heavens. Then I stared in horror, my hand to my mouth, as it began to spiral slowly down – and crashed into the garden next door…

Fortunately, the aircraft that came to temporary grief was a powered model, but it was a magnificent piece of engineering, with a 2ft wingspan. It had been designed and made for me by my father, Desmond Naismith, when I was five years old. It was the most wonderful present I had ever had, and I was utterly enchanted by it. I'm sure it inspired my subsequent passion for flying, along with all the thrilling tales told to me by my father and aunt, both of whom were pilots.

We had been flying the plane in our garden in Hampstead, north London, but my father decided to take it on to the Heath so that we could try it out over a longer distance. When it crashed I was sent to retrieve it from the tree where it had landed, in the garden belonging to our neighbour, Derwent Hall Caine, and to apologise. My father brought up the rear! Our family was friendly with the actor and Labour politician, who was later knighted, and one of his maids, Eva, used to come and wash up for us during the Second World War, when we had fewer staff. However, despite our cordial relations, he was furious at what he saw as an invasion of his privacy when my little plane landed on his property, so it was all somewhat embarrassing!

My father was a test pilot and engineer and he used to take me flying from Hendon airfield, even though it wasn't officially allowed. I remember I wore a type of tracksuit for the trips. He was an extremely clever man, a fact that I didn't fully appreciate until I was older. He worked for Vickers and De Havilland and later designed the hangars and all-weather runway at Goose Bay, in Labrador, Canada. For VE day and VJ day, he redesigned the fountains in Trafalgar Square to spout out red, white and blue water. My aunt, his sister Paddy Naismith, was one of the first women pilots. She used to ferry Ramsay MacDonald, the Labour prime minister, around. Paddy was a good pilot but not such a good navigator and used to fly low so that she could find out where she was by reading the signboards on railway stations. When an alarmed MacDonald once queried why they were flying so close to the ground, she told him it was due to "inclement" weather conditions, even though it was a bright, sunny day!

My mother, Elizabeth, was very beautiful and was known as the best-dressed woman in London society. She was a great socialite and knew many people. She was interested in flying because of my father and one day, while attending a ball, she spoke to the

Prince of Wales about it. He said he had a plane that he kept at Hendon, a two-seater Gypsy Moth. He asked her if she would like to go in it and she said yes. I remember her telling me about the flight, but we didn't make a big thing of her going flying with the future king. I think I was more interested in hearing about the plane!

I was born – on January 28, 1934 – into privilege, but it was only in later years that I realised quite how cosseted I was. My mother's father, Fritz Dupre, was French. He was an elegant, impeccably dressed man who always wore a stiff white collar. He had a lovely smile and would sit me on his knee in his swivel desk chair and we would whirl round and round. He was a very clever man and was articulate in three languages. He could be extremely amusing and was a very good husband. He made his fortune by importing iron, manganese and ore and was driven to his offices in St Mary Axe in the City every day by his chauffeur. He had a vast, beautiful Georgian house, The Firs, with acres of grounds, in Spaniards Road by Hampstead Heath. You could see across London from the garden, including St Paul's Cathedral. I can still remember the telephone number at the house: Speedwell 3083.

The five-acre garden backed on to the renowned Spaniards Inn. A Spaniard was reputedly buried in the grounds of The Firs, in a grave surrounded by iron railings. He was supposed to have been interred along with some treasure, possibly from the Armada, and people were sometimes caught by the gardeners or chauffeurs attempting to dig it up. I believe the police were even called on occasion. There was a tunnel from The Firs to the inn and the entrance was situated near the boiler room, in the basement. Grandpa had it bricked up but we could venture down it a little way – quite thrilling for us as children!

I was born at The Firs and brought up there, together with my cousins Ann and David, who were the children of my Uncle Jimmy by his first marriage. It was a large household. My grandparents had eight children, several of whom continued to live at home. They were all clever, trilingual people. My mother was the only one to go to school, the others had governesses. My aunts Helen – "Mim" – and Anna lived with us. Uncle Walter became a famous judge. He was Chief Justice in Cyprus when Archbishop Makarios was a powerful figure. He then travelled all over the world and I later stayed with his family when I was living in Canada. My aunt Ella was a concert organist. She lived in Mayfield, Sussex and played in the church there for many years.

Uncle Jimmy helped to run the family business. Sadly Eric died, aged 16, before I was born but the tragedy was rarely discussed and I know little about him. Walter, Jimmy and Peter, the youngest, all went to Downing College, Cambridge and we went to visit Peter there in Grandpa's Rolls-Royce. He became a doctor and went to work at

Charing Cross Hospital, where he met his future wife, a nurse named Elizabeth. They often visited The Firs and, fortunately, were there on the occasion when PB, my step-brother, fell from the top floor.

His fall was broken by iron railings and Peter and Elizabeth used an ironing board as a stretcher for him. PB was unconscious for two weeks and we thought he would never recover. When he did come round, he was told he could have whatever he wanted, and he said he would like a banana. As rationing was in force, Aunt Ella went to a fruit auction and bought one for £5!

Peter and Elizabeth eventually moved to a lovely house in Hemel Hempstead, where they organised wonderful family firework parties, and then to a large house with acres of land called Windleshaw. When my aunt became ill I used to go and help with the children, Helen, Nicky, Pierre and Richard. My uncle loved animals and kept pigs and ponies. He had a pony and trap and I used to take the children to school in it. When I married he gave me the trap and the beautiful leather harness, which I have always treasured.

Uncle Peter became the medical officer at Gatwick Airport. He influenced my interest in medicine, which was to play such a large part in my life. My cousin, Nicky, eventually died but, fortunately, I was able to do all I could to help him while he was ill.

My grandfather had built on to The Firs as his children came along. At one stage a beautiful ballroom was added where wonderful parties were held and an orchestra played in the special area that had been designed for them. At Christmas a huge tree covered with tiny candles soared right up to the ceiling. At Easter, chocolate egg hunts were organised for us around the grounds.

We had a very large staff, including a butler called James, two chambermaids, my German grandmother Else's personal maid, Alice, and a scullery maid, plus Cook, kitchen staff and an under-butler who did the heavy work around the house and tended the huge boiler room – The Firs had full central heating, which was almost unheard of then. James and one of the kitchen staff served us at mealtimes. Although we were waited on, there was a lot of kindness in the household. The staff were treated very well and had excellent accommodation. My grandfather extended the cottage lived in by Mr Barrett, the head gardener, when his wife was expecting a child. We were allowed into the servants' quarters occasionally, when they had celebrations, and loved to watch them dance.

Every morning at 11 my grandmother and I would go into the kitchen and have a cup of cocoa with Cook, sitting at the lovely old kitchen table. My grandmother would then go off to discuss the day's catering arrangements with her. I still have Cook's special old wooden chair. She was German and, when the war came, she told my grandmother: "Don't worry, Madam. They won't bomb us. I'm German!" During the war, she taught Grandma to cook and she became extremely competent.

On the third floor of the house there was a small butler's pantry where the water was heated to be taken in jugs to the washstands in the bedrooms. Food for the indoor pets was prepared there, too, and I used to help out and was taught how to wash up their dishes properly by my aunt Mim.

We had a lot of animals at The Firs, which I loved — they all helped to make my early childhood idyllic. My aunt Helen had a mare that she used to ride side-saddle. I had a Cairn terrier named Janey. Aunt Helen also had four geese, Matthew, Mark, Luke and John. Aunt Ella had a monkey that used to slide down the banisters in The Firs and, if it took a dislike to someone, would jump on them! There was also a tortoise called Cornelius, whose house was underneath the conservatory where tropical fruit was grown. This was next to the billiard room and all the beautiful garden furniture was kept in a store underneath that.

The children had a schoolroom and a playroom at The Firs, but we loved to hide in an alcove in my mother's bedroom. I remember my grandmother had a little boudoir. She had a beautiful, small table in there with a secret drawer that my grandfather had made from a cherry tree in his garden in Germany and it is now one of my most treasured possessions. I was a tomboy and loved to spend time climbing trees in the garden. Girls didn't have shorts in those days, so I made my father buy me some that were designed for boys!

I had a pony, which I used to ride around the large grounds of The Firs. However, there were certain parts of the garden where I was not supposed to go on horseback. If I transgressed the gardeners told the head gardener, Mr Barrett, or my grandmother and I got into trouble — the staff didn't feel able to reprimand "Miss Diana" themselves. I became a very competent rider and later, when I was about 10 or 11, I would set off across London, alone, on my pony to visit Aunt Julie at her home in Camden Hill — she had a field and a barn where I would turn my pony out during my stay. No one would dream of allowing a child to do that now, there would be far too much traffic and other dangers.

As well as being told off for riding my pony in the no-go areas of the gardens, I remember getting into hot water on one occasion when I was angry with my Uncle Jimmy over something. I can't remember what it was now but I know I kicked him on the shins — he grabbed me and put me across his knee and gave me the hiding of my life.

I must have inherited my mischievous side from my mother – as a child she was apparently a great prankster. The vicar used to enjoy coming to tea once a week in those days and on one occasion when he was expected she strung black cotton in between the wrought-iron gates at the entrance to the house. It was raining and the vicar and his umbrella became dreadfully tangled up! My mother got into terrible trouble and was sent to her room by my grandmother. She had to apologise but was forgiven. She had a very infectious laugh, inherited by my half-sister, Lorna.

My mother had a great friend, Joy, and when they attended balls and dances in grand hotels they would search out the large, wheeled laundry baskets and push each other along the corridors. If anyone came along, whoever was pushing would throw a sheet over the basket, leaving the "rider" inside, and walk nonchalantly away!

Joy later married Peter de Havilland, who was on the business side of the aviation family. We knew his brother, Geoffrey, who was tragically killed while testing a new aircraft for the company. We used to watch him fly and I remember being instructed to write a letter of condolence when he died. Both men were very striking.

Mummy was also friendly with the renowned entertainers, Webster Booth and Anne Ziegler. They lived in Hampstead and my mother would visit them and listen to Anne playing and to them both singing. Lorna has the photograph of them that they gave to my mother.

Sadly, my idyllic childhood was rocked by the end of my parents' marriage. When necessary, our family's animals had been looked after by a brilliant and extremely handsome vet named Proby Cautley – he was one of several who tended the Queen's pets and horses, although he was very discreet and never spoke about it. He also advised the Royal Zoological Society, which was responsible for London Zoo.

My mother fell in love with Proby. She left my father and they were divorced, which was far more shocking in those days than it is today and, naturally, devastating for me in many ways. Her situation meant, for instance, that she wasn't allowed to present me at court, as my grandmother, who had also been presented, had done for her.

My mother subsequently studied at the Royal Veterinary College and became her new husband's anaesthetist. He had a practice in Wellington Road, St John's Wood, and I spent some time there while growing up. Through this new relationship I acquired my half-sister, Lorna, and step-brother, PB. He eventually took over his grandparents' printing company, Posener, Walter and Harris, in Shoe Lane, opposite the old *Daily Express* building in Fleet Street, and became a wealthy man.

After the divorce I believe my father returned to his family at Muswell Hill. My grandmother helped to bring me up, together with Aunt Helen and my nanny, Miss

K Wall. I never knew her first name and addressed her as Miss Wall but I loved her very much. I was eventually sent to school, with my cousin Ann, to St Margarets, in Hampstead. The headmistress was called Miss Coppinger. One of the pupils was Jennifer Gail, who was the first girl to be on television. She appeared with Mrs Mills and Muffin the Mule, which was very popular then.

I loved my grandmother dearly. She was kind, elegant and clever and much admired by the staff. She was very keen for her children to learn German, her native tongue, and she was aided in this by one of Grandpa's sisters, Tante Ena, who lived in his house in Germany and used to come to stay with us.

My grandmother was a wonderful hostess and gave many grand dinner parties. She imposed a strict regime: good manners were essential and we had to rise politely if anyone came into the room and to curtsey when necessary. Punctuality at mealtimes was insisted upon and a huge gong was employed to ensure that we were on time – once to warn us to go to the dining room within the next five minutes and a second time to tell us we should be there *NOW*! We always changed into smart, formal afternoon clothes for tea. The Firs had a vast dining room and I was allowed to sit next to my grandmother as I was the youngest. Generally we children were supposed to be seen and not heard.

This training served me well when a very special guest was invited to The Firs. My grandmother had become a friend of Queen Mary and one day she came to tea and I was presented to her. She arrived in a Daimler with just a chauffeur and lady's maid in attendance. The door was opened to Her Majesty by James, the butler, and my grandmother welcomed her and took her into our exquisite drawing room. I gathered from Grandma that Queen Mary didn't like fussy food, so she was offered simple fare – cucumber sandwiches and small cakes, such as a plain sponge, which I was allowed to finish up in the nursery afterwards. I was taken to meet her by Nanny, who was not presented. We came in from the ballroom entrance to the drawing room. I had been told to curtsey at a distance of six feet, which I did. The Queen held out her hand and said: "Hello, my dear." Although suitably daunted, I managed to reply: "Good afternoon, Ma'am", as I had been instructed. Then I took three steps back and was returned to the nursery.

I don't remember having a special dress for the occasion. As we always had to change for tea anyway I had several good dresses, usually plain but beautifully cut, often with smocking, which I always wore with pristine white socks and shoes. A lot of my clothes came from Harrods and we went on shopping expeditions there in my grandfather's beautiful Rolls – the number was AUU3 and it seated eight. (We also had a Daimler and, on informal trips, I was sometimes allowed to sit beside the chauffeur.) We would draw up outside the front door and, after we had got out, the chauffeur would drive off and park. When we had completed our shopping, a lady's maid was despatched to fetch him and he would return to collect us. I was allowed to visit the toy department in Harrods but wasn't bought toys all the time, like children are now. They were reserved for Christmas and birthdays. However, my father did buy me white ice skates when I was about five or six – a very special present – and he took me to Queens ice rink and taught me to skate. We went alone, without Nanny – a rare occurrence and very exciting.

Scandal rocked our comfortable world once more when my aunt Anna fell in love with my grandfather's chauffeur. She had been schooled at The Firs by a governess and was clever and spoke three languages. However, I believe she was lonely and she would go to the garages to talk to one of the drivers, Jo Millns. The chauffeurs and their wives had excellent accommodation in a very pretty mews block in the grounds, where the cars were also kept. The men were excellent drivers and Rolls-Royce trained them to maintain the vehicles as well as to drive them before placing them with its clients.

Anna would tell my grandmother she was just walking in the grounds when she went to visit Millns but, one day, Grandma went to talk to the chauffeurs about something and found her daughter in her lover's arms. Anna was in fact pregnant with my cousin, Joan. The couple had "disgraced the family", so my grandfather insisted they marry and sent them to South Africa, where he had many contacts. Anna had a second child, William, there. Eventually the family returned home and my grandfather bought them a house in Eastbourne but I don't think things turned out too well.

Our family had a choice of holiday homes. My grandfather owned several other houses, the spacious Turret Lodge in Frinton – it had its own beach hut, which he loved – which is now a hotel, and two in Germany. The one that we used to visit, Haus Dupre in Johannisberg, was a *schloss* and we children had our own wing, shared with nannies and governesses. I remember my grandmother had the most beautiful bathroom there. She used to buy a special ceramic tile at every place she visited and then had them fixed to the wall. They made a stunning display.

My grandfather knew a lot of people locally and we had the run of the village. He was a great wine connoisseur and the estate had its own seven-acre vineyard; the wine was brought back to England in a hogshead and bottled here. It was a hock and cost five shillings to produce a bottle. I still have one, which I am keeping for posterity! His other property was at Wiesbaden, but it was bombed during the war and I never went there. We would set off for our holiday destinations in the Daimler or the Rolls with James, the butler, Alice, Grandma's maid, and Cook. There was always a skeleton staff kept at the houses. If we were going to Europe, we travelled by boat and car.

My childhood was rudely interrupted again by the war. We were in Germany when we heard the news that the Second World War was breaking out, but managed to get back to England in time. Alice, Grandma's maid, had married a German, Hans Klaus, but he had to remain in Germany and, tragically, she never saw him again.

Back at home my uncle Jimmy became an air-raid warden and we children wore tin hats, pretending to be important. He taught us to put out incendiary bombs using the buckets of sand that were kept around the house. Butterfly bombs landed in the trees and another type of bomb landed on our croquet lawn; the next day we went out collecting shrapnel. An incendiary bomb also landed on the roof of The Firs. Fortunately, they were all dealt with without any harm being done. The ARP meetings were held at nearby Kenwood House and I'm afraid it was all a bit "Dad's Army". Uncle Jimmy rode a bike with his regulation gun attached to it and one day came back looking rather bedraggled after he cycled straight into a pit – a fact that he preferred to hide by saying: "I just fell off my bike."! Uncle Jimmy was also involved in looking after the family company and Uncle Peter, who still worked as a doctor, was not called up. My aunts did voluntary work at New End hospital. We had to cut down on staff: we were allowed a chauffeur, one cook, one maid and Alice, plus two gardeners. Much of our home-grown produce was given to the hospital. Our own food was rationed – in the dining room we all had our own butter dishes and were each allowed 3oz per week. Uncle Jimmy used to try to bribe me to part with mine!

One of the rooms in the huge basement at The Firs was turned into an air-raid shelter. We took the leaves out of the dining room table and put camp beds on them. There was a shaft down into the shelter from the garden, which we would have had to use to escape if we were bombed – we used to enjoy sliding down it. The staff came with us into the shelter and we had sandwiches and Thermos flasks of tea and water in case we had to stay down there for any length of time.

My mother rented Brickhouse Farm in Sandhurst, Kent, for a while, so that we could decamp there when she felt life in London was becoming too dangerous. The farmhouse was old and lit by oil lamps and I remember spending time there with her and my cousin, David.

Life at The Firs changed tragically in 1941 with the death of my grandfather. He had been out to dinner at the Dorchester and had a heart attack as he negotiated the revolving doors in the hotel, as he was leaving to return home. My aunt Julie was there, too, and she told me what had happened. Women didn't go to funerals then, so I didn't get a real chance to say goodbye to my beloved Grandpa, who had provided me with such love and security. He was laid to rest in the family vault in Highgate Cemetery.

My grandmother was devastated by his death. She developed bad headaches and I used to sit with her and rub cool cologne on her forehead and temples. But, with typical stoicism, she carried on running the house with the family and the business continued, too, under the care of my uncle Jimmy. Life didn't change too greatly I suppose, but, without the central, towering presence of Grandpa, his smile, his humour, intelligence and love, The Firs was never quite the same again.

My Secret Postwar Mission

From a child's point of view, the war was quite exciting but my biggest adventure came immediately afterwards, when I was about 12. My Uncle Schubert was the American Consul in Munich. Because of his position he managed to obtain a special visa for me and I was the first of my family to go back to Germany, where we had spent such happy holidays with Grandpa and Grandma in the Thirties. But this time I was on a special mission. My grandmother's sister was struggling financially because of the war and I was elected to take some money to her.

I had far more than the allowance but because I was only young it was thought that no one would suspect me. I had German marks in my little handbag and my suitcase. My grandmother told me what was going to happen and said: "Be normal!" I flew to Munich and at the airport had to show my special, rather important-looking papers that Uncle Schubert had organised for me. The passport official asked if I had any money but I deflected the question by saying I was going to stay with my aunt and uncle. I didn't lie!

Uncle Schubert's glamorous wife, Aunt Gilly, who was my father's sister, picked me up in her own car and drove me to their lovely house. She later took me to see my relations, who were obviously no longer very well off. They had buried their family silver in the garden during the war and wept when they saw the money I had brought. They had made a huge apple strudel to celebrate our visit and we took some home with us, wrapped in greaseproof paper. Aunt Gilly warned me to be gracious about the dish as the family had probably had to save up to provide it for us.

My German relatives were very keen to get me to speak the language. One of the sons, Pieter Hecker, was fluent in Russian and had spied for England during the war.

I saw a lot of devastation in the country, the result of Allied bombing, but I have happy memories, too. There was an amazing clock on one building, the Muenchner Rathhaus, in Munich. Every evening at 9pm the figure of a night watchman appears, followed by his dog, and travels round from the left to the right. Shortly after that the figure of a child, the Muenchner Kindl, appears from the right, followed by the Angel of Peace, and circles to the left. The little performance, accompanied by the Cradle Song from Brahms, lasts for two minutes and signifies that it is time all children were in bed. I was captivated by the scene and my aunt bought me a beautiful charm for my bracelet depicting it. I was taken to see the famous passion play at Oberammergau, where the local men grew their beards specially to take part in it. I also went riding in the forest, which I loved.

My aunt was a leading light in the American Red Cross and had her uniforms made by Dior. She used to put on shows and parties for the American troops in Germany with other members of the organisation. I desperately wanted to go but was not allowed to – people were much stricter about what children could see in those days and it was past my bedtime. But she used to dress up and rehearse at home while I watched – I have vivid memories of her dancing the Can-Can!

The Cautleys

My step-father came from an illustrious family that was descended from Edward I and numbered many of the leading professions among its distinguished ranks, including medicine, the clergy, the military and engineers. One, also named Proby, was a 19th century pioneer in canal building and was responsible for the Ganges Canal, one of the largest irrigation canals ever built. The Cautleys were also writers, publishers, scholars and poets and the family has branches all over the world.

My second husband, Robin Patten, to whom I have now been married for 40 years, my son, Jamie, my step-brother PB and I all attended a family reunion in 1986 in Cautley in Cumbria, which has obvious family connections. It was a remarkable gathering with members from all over the world. There was a celebration lunch and church service and some of us then attempted to walk up to Cautley Spout, a waterfall set in a lovely valley. It turned out to be a very steep climb. PB made it to the top, while Robin and I got some of the way and then made the descent mainly on our bottoms!

The Firs, our family home in Hampstead Heath, showing the conservatory and billiard room

Grandma, Grandpa and Uncle Peter outside the Firs

Mummy outside the family home with a typically stylish car

The Firs with my mother's car parked in front

Safe in my darling Daddy's arms

*Even when tiny
I was a tomboy with bandaged knees*

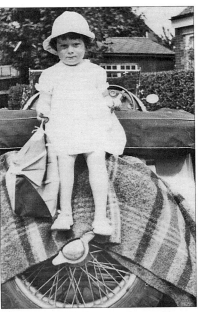

*Posing on Uncle Jimmy's rare sports
Bentley during a picnic*

I loved the playhouse that Grandma had specially built for me

Gardening with Mummy - in my beloved boys' shorts!

A studio portrait of me in my upmarket riding outfit!

Turret Lodge, our holiday home at Frinton

Grandpa's turreted home in Germany where we spent wonderful holidays

The Prince of Wales's plane in which Mummy went flying with the future King

A portrait of my distinguished Grandpa

*A remarkable portrait of Aunt Gilly in her Red Cross uniform handmade by Dior,
repairing her make-up in the ruined remains of Hitler's house in Germany*

Debs and Other Delights

Eventually the time came for me to lead a less sheltered existence and I was sent to Francis Holland School in Regent's Park. My cousins, Ann and David, were sent to Malvern and Felsted. We had a governess at home, Miss James, who became a great friend of my mother. She had a child and my mother was very good to her.

I travelled unaccompanied to my new school and caught the 210 bus from The Firs to Golders Green and then another on to Baker Street. The school was on a corner there. It was huge, with a beautiful galleried hall, where we had prayers every morning, and an inner courtyard that had a netball court. For other games, we walked in a crocodile to Regent's Park, where we played lacrosse and tennis. One day I broke a tooth in a particularly lively match. Fortunately, my step-father Proby's brother, Ronald, was a brilliant dental surgeon and I was whisked off to his practice and he managed to fix it for me. (Later he expertly rebuilt my mother's jaw after she was injured in a car crash when someone drove into Proby's MG. I had to go to the surgery at Guy's Hospital so that they could compare the formation of my jaw with my mother's. This could have been a real tragedy because my mother was a real beauty, but Uncle Ronald's expertise and that of the surgeons at Guy's saved her looks.)

I was very sporty, but academically lazy. My mother, somewhat inadvisably, had told me I didn't need to worry about education because I wouldn't have to work – she took it for granted that I would marry someone wealthy. She kept on saying: "Oh, don't bother", and I probably took her at her word! However, I was good at art and also maths, although I'm not now. No one really discussed careers with us in those days but at some stage I thought I might like to do medicine and began to make more effort with my studies. In the last two years at Francis Holland I really started to work; I even came top in maths. My reports gradually began to improve but I didn't get my School Certificate until I went to the Chatelard, a Swiss finishing school.

One of my classmates at Francis Holland was the actress Joan Collins; her sister, the writer, Jackie, was also there. I remember they were both great fun. I had a reunion with Joan when she did a one-woman show in Hastings and I bought front-row tickets. I had written to her at the theatre beforehand and, during the interval, her husband, Percy, came out and found me. We met in her dressing-room later and talked over old times.

Most of my fellow pupils came from wealthy families but they all loved coming to the parties I was allowed to have in the ballroom at The Firs. They would arrive with their parents, chauffeurs or in taxis and they didn't want to leave! We had music on a radiogram. Once, it broke down and my cousin David played the grand piano so that we could carry on dancing. The ballroom had concertinaed doors and the food was laid out in the dining room next to it. We would have a fairly plain buffet, perhaps a whole ham, which was carved, with a German potato salad – Cook and my grandmother being German. It was made with milk, vinegar and herbs and was delicious. We also had trifle and thought we were terribly grown-up!

I remember getting my first long dress for one of Ann's parties, when I was 15. It was blue taffeta, with puff sleeves and a tight bodice, and I had shoes with little, tiny heels.

My mother wanted me to attend a boarding school, so I then moved to The Downs at Seaford. I didn't like it very much but I loved the uniform – we wore cloaks that we could wrap ourselves up in on the way to church. However, the headmistress, Miss Pitt, was also the games mistress and as I was so keen on sport, we got on quite well. I liked lacrosse and netball and, because we had had a grass court at The Firs, I was quite good at tennis. As a child I never told anyone that my great-uncle, James Naismith, had in fact invented basketball; you just didn't say things like that.

I had skied from an early age; my mother used to take me regularly to Adelboden, in Switzerland. On one occasion we went with the Foreman family. My mother was very friendly with "Aunt Gladys", and her nephew, Michael, who became an agricultural merchant, was one of my first boyfriends. We went to church on Sunday in Switzerland and Michael and I had to share a single Bible to read the lessons, over which we had some amiable squabbles!

My skiing prowess came in extremely useful when I moved from The Downs to my finishing school in Switzerland. I had a wonderful year there; I could see Mont Blanc from my dormitory window. The headmistress was called Miss Bragginton. She had very large feet and had to wear special shoes, and so we tended to look at those rather than her face.

I gained my School Certificate and skied for the Chatelard against other local English schools, winning several plaques. Our games mistress was known as Little Mo and I could out-ski her – I could out-ski all of them! We often used to go to the resort of Gstaad where the conditions were better. It was beautiful – in those days it was just a tiny little village. I also played ice hockey; won a cup for table tennis and won most things in house tennis matches. In winter, the tennis courts would be flooded and we would skate on them instead.

One of my friends, Beatrice, was related to King Farouk. I still have a little ivory elephant that she gave to me, probably after I helped her with her skating or something like that.

We were taught social skills but also practical ones. I learnt to make white sauces and how to mash potatoes with a fork. I was even instructed on the correct way to clean a bath – we were told to use an old flannel on which we had to put a loop and to keep it on a hook for the purpose! Although I came from a very privileged background, and it was assumed I would marry into money and would never need any of these skills, I was a fairly practical, down-to-earth girl and never afraid of hard work. I just rolled up my sleeves and got on with it all.

Once a term a dance would be organised with boys from nearby schools. Our names were put into a hat and the boys' names were put into another and there would be a draw to choose our dancing partners.

These halcyon days were sadly interrupted by the death of my beloved grandmother. Miss Bragginton called me into her study one day and said she had very sad news. I was desperately upset. My mother wrote to say that Grandma had died very peacefully. Apparently, my step-father, Proby, had been able to get oxygen to help treat her; it was hard to get hold of in those days. There was little communication then, so I couldn't even telephone home. Once again, I just had to get on with it.

During the school vacations I had wonderful working holidays, which helped to inspire my love of the countryside and animals. I also learnt quite a lot about veterinary science. Through my step-father I had a "pseudo uncle", known as "Heavy" Peace. He was also a vet and had a practice and a farm near Dorking. Both his sons became vets, eventually establishing a leading horse clinic at Newmarket. I helped in the practice, cleaning out the kennels, and mucked out the horses on the farm and helped to harrow the fields, often driving the tractor. I had learnt to drive in the grounds of The Firs as a small child and could drive anything as I grew up. I improved my riding in Surrey, too.

In Hereford, on another vacation, I stayed with a friend of my father's, near Leominster. Her farm had no electricity or running water, which was quite a change for me. We used to cut the bracken for bedding with a scythe – it was extremely hard work but I was strong so it wasn't too arduous for me.

When I stayed at Colonel Butler's farm in Chalfont St Peter, Bucks, I learnt to milk 40 goats by hand! We used to separate it and send the cream in churns up to London by train. The village had a beautiful cricket ground and my step-father would come down at weekends to play; he was a wicket-keeper and captained a Sunday side. Geoffrey, my step-father's friend, would be the umpire and cheat like mad! All kinds of famous cricketers would turn up to play, including Denis Compton and Sir Learie Constantine, who was utterly charming and a real gentleman.

My aunt Mim had two cottages: Rose Cottage, in Sandy Lane, Selbourne, Hants, and Peartree Cottage, at Harcombe, near Hailsham. We often visited Selbourne. The cottage was by the golf course and we took the laundry across it to a woman we nicknamed Mrs Tiggywinkle. We had a great time outdoors there and I was taught to saw up wood. Aunt Mim's car was a Morris, EGW 603. I saw it years later and offered to buy it back for her.

In later life, Aunt Mim married her neighbour at Peartree Cottage, John Budd. He lived next door to Airey Neave, the Conservative MP who was killed when the IRA planted a bomb under his car at the House of Commons. My first husband, Chris Freeman, was best man at the wedding and I did the catering.

On my return to England from school in Switzerland the time came for me to be presented at court, as both my grandmother and mother had been. The regulations were strict and, as I said, my mother was not allowed to present me as she was divorced. My Aunt Julie, my father's sister, also a debutante, did so instead; it had to be a relation or someone who knew the family very well. My aunt never married but had two wonderful boyfriends, whom she used to play off against each other! She used to buy and sell property, and did so very successfully.

Girls paired up for the ceremony and the attendant celebrations. My partner was Diana Plunkett, with whom I had been at the Chatelard, who was extremely good-looking. We went shopping together for our gowns. I was quite sad that times had changed and I could not wear one of the dresses that my mother and grandmother had been presented in. They had carried traditional white feathers and looked stunning in the portraits that were done of them. However, it was fun touring the stores with my friend. I looked at a lot of dresses before making my decision. I think my gown came from Fenwick in the end. It was pale blue, quite classic, and my shoes were white, with heels. Diana chose something that was much too revealing to start with, but I managed to talk her out of it! Her final choice was a classic style in pale pink and she looked really striking. We were trying to be sophisticated and grown up so wore very subtle make-up that we applied ourselves.

It was all very exciting but I wasn't particularly nervous. I had grown up being taught how to behave in all kinds of illustrious company and, of course, the former Queen had come to tea at The Firs, so I wasn't overawed by the occasion.

We arrived in the courtyard at Buckingham Palace in a hired car – Aunt Julie didn't drive. Then we went up the steps and into the main hall. Along a corridor, towards the end, was the magnificent room where the presentation took place. We lined up and our supporters gave our names which were read out aloud. We were presented individually to the Queen – it was Elizabeth II by then; she was young and lovely – and we had to curtsey. We then all remained in the room, allowing the Queen to leave first. It was an impressive occasion, not least because I was seeing the inside of the palace for the first time. It was very beautiful and elegant with high, floor-length Georgian windows. It was stunning but it seemed to me much like The Firs, albeit much larger and grander.

There were various events linked to the presentation. Some of the debutantes went out for a meal together afterwards at Claridge's. We all went to the traditional Queen Charlotte's Ball and each had two balls of our own. I had one at Grosvenor House and another at the Bagatelle club. Edmundo Ross's famous Latin-American orchestra played on that occasion; he was a friend of my step-father. He had a little Scottie and my step-father looked after it. Ross was supposed to be a ladies' man but he was charming to me and Diana.

There were some privileges attached to being a debutante that were worth having: you could sign a book of condolence if a member of the Royal Family was ill and, on board ship, you could pull rank and sit at the Captain's table!

It was during my teens that I did quite a lot of modelling. I showed clothes for Lady in Black, which became Mareusa, and Susan Small at fashion shows. My mother had a dress shop in Hanover Square called Peta, after a friend of mine from the Chatelard. (In later years I modelled for Rose-Anne in Rye, in fashion shows all over Sussex.)

I did enjoy wearing lovely clothes and being very feminine, but, as I mentioned, I was basically a tomboy – quite an unconventional person – and keen on practical projects, rather than dolls, from an early age. I was mad on cars but had a motorbike initially, before I got a driving licence at 16. My first car was an Austin 7. I had to build it myself as Mummy wouldn't let me have one until I could mend it. My "Uncle" Clive Claremont, a friend of my father, did precision engineering and I learnt a tremendous amount from him about maintaining and repairing cars. He built his own car, the Claremont, in which I won the Brighton Speed Trials. I was mad on racing and had applied for my own licence. It was a thrilling experience.

Through Uncle Clive I became friendly with the racing driver Peter Gammon, whose family owned the old, well-known Guildford drapery store, and I used to do his pit stops for him. I suppose it was an unusual thing for a girl to do but I didn't think about that, I just got on with it. There were other girls around but they were frightfully glamorous and didn't do a lot; I suppose I was regarded as one of the boys. The cars had to be roadsters but Peter modified a single-decker bus to carry his MG, using ramps to get it in and out. We would drive to a spot about five miles away from whatever track we were visiting and then I would drive the car from there, so at least it had been on the road for a while *en route*.

I also helped Bill Mason who had the most beautiful, open green sports Bentley with a leather strap round the bonnet. We used to practise pit stops before races, jacking the car up and changing the wheels – we knocked them on with a mallet in those days. I was surrounded by dirty rags and often used to get covered in oil, but Swarfega, in my case, turned out to be a girl's best friend! The cars were always scrutinised before the races to ensure they were safe to go out. I found that fascinating and was proud that we were never rejected. We did the pit stops in minutes then, but today it's all over in a matter of seconds.

I would roar round the circuits in my own car if I got the chance – you could get away with anything then. I took my racing licence when I subsequently moved to Canada, but raced my much-cherished XK140, which I bought out there, only once; I was too worried about anything happening to it.

I also used to help to grind in valves and balance con rods for Colin Chapman, who founded Lotus cars. I went on test drives of the Lotuses up the M1 – there was no speed limit then. Several of us would follow in a security vehicle. On one occasion the front suspension went on a car. I was wearing an old-fashioned riding mac and Colin said: "I'll have that belt, Diana," and he "bodged up" the suspension temporarily with it!

Colin was a great character and had a reputation for being something of a high liver. However, while he was working he was extremely professional. There were some parties at his works but I never saw anything untoward. His wife seemed to me to be very forbearing, though, and took a lot from him. What Colin wanted, Colin got…

Uncle Clive invented the wishbone front suspension but he never patented it and Lotus went on to incorporate it into its cars. Coming back from France not so long ago I saw a Lotus on the ferry and told the owner that it had wishbone suspension. He obviously knew nothing about it and was quite taken aback when this older lady started talking about it with some authority, but I explained that I was one of the very first people to know about it.

During my teens I had grown fond of cricket. My step-father's home was opposite Lord's ground and I could lean out of my bedroom window there and see the scoreboard. I used to play squash at Lord's and after one game I met two nice men, Toby Pain and John Lyle. John and I had a lot in common and he asked me to go out with him. For the first time in my life I fell madly in love and we had the most wonderful time together. His parents had a beautiful house, Shore Hill, at Kemsing and I had my own room there. John was one of the heirs to Tate & Lyle, although I didn't realise that for some time, and the house was known locally as Treacle Towers. John's parents were very fond of me and I of them. He had an amazing car, a Bristol 301, which I loved. After I had raced the Claremont at the Brighton speed trials, Uncle Clive let me drive it to Shore Hill *en route* to his home at Muswell Hill. John had some influential people staying that weekend and I arrived in it in great style. John showed the car off to his guests and was very proud of me!

John was handsome. He used to call me Monk; I can't remember why, but we all had nicknames then. He had two children from his first marriage, Christopher and Wendy, and I used to love to bowl for them in endless games of cricket at Shorehill. John and I also enjoyed driving and swimming together

However, I was 17 and John was 12 years older and my mother said the age difference was too great and I couldn't marry him. We were devastated but one didn't disobey one's parents in those days and we were forced to separate. His parents were very upset about it, too. I kept in touch with his mother until she died. There wasn't any bad feeling between our families because of my mother's edict. They all eventually met when I returned from Canada and Mummy gave a ball so that I could see all my friends again.

John and I kept in touch and John gave me a watch, engraved with the words: "Monk. All love, John." I was desperately upset when it was later stolen while I was staying with my aunt in Hampstead. But he also gave me a Parker pen and pencil set engraved with my initials that I still have to this day.

After our enforced break-up I was distraught. It was then that my mother decided I should go to Canada where we had relatives. And so, with a heavy heart, I packed my bags and set off miles away across the Atlantic …

*My grandmother,
typically elegant as a debutante*

*Mummy in her beautiful
coming out gown*

Canadian Capers

John drove me to Liverpool in his Bristol to take the ship to Montreal. I missed him dreadfully during the voyage but I had a reasonable cabin and enjoyed the crossing as much as I could. There were pastimes such as dancing and table tennis to divert me and, of course, as a debutante I was treated with great respect and I had the right to sit at the Captain's table or, if that was full, I could dine with the doctor or the purser.

My family knew some people in Canada and I had a few connections there. When my Uncle Walter was in Alberta with his family I stayed with them. My father eventually moved to Canada and lectured at Toronto University; we saw each other from time to time and he helped me to buy my beloved XK140. He met a young American called Helen at the university, who was studying to be a concert pianist and singer, and they later married and lived in Toronto. They eventually moved to Costa Mesa in America, and lived in an old wooden house, next to a peach orchard, that was owned by Helen's family. My father was intensely practical – a bit of a boffin – and he redesigned and replumbed the property. I remember Helen being annoyed when he turned the water off!

My father carried on designing – he created the first cycle helmet but never patented it. He was quite eccentric. He was brilliant with words and would often return my letters to him corrected! I had a half-sister, Vivian, and she had a daughter, Rebecca, now in her teens. Her son, Christopher, tragically died. My father and Helen later moved to a new property in Irvine, California.

My children, Jamie and Elizabeth, often visited my father and his new family when they first moved to America and Elizabeth in particular loved it there. After she finished at her school, Beresford House in Eastbourne, where she became head girl and was renowned for her sporting successes in tennis and riding, she wanted to go to university in the United States. She gained five O-levels and two A-levels but hadn't got high enough grades in English to qualify. We were living in Suffolk by that time, following my divorce from Chris, the children's father, and my remarriage to Robin, and she improved her grades there and eventually went to Orange Coast College in California to study a wide variety of subjects, including art, architecture and aviation, with which my father helped her, and pre-med. (Elizabeth had picked up a lot of medical knowledge, as I had, through farming and mixing with the vets in the family and could lamb a ewe at a very early age. She always had lovely hands – people called them healing hands. She now lives with her partner in California and has made a great success of her medical career.)

29

My great-uncle, James Naismith, was born in Ontario. He invented basketball in 1891 and this earned him all kinds of posthumous honours. There are several statues of him in the country. I saw one in Montreal and went to an exhibition in Toronto where there was a stand providing information about him. I have a book about his life and he was obviously a fascinating man; perhaps I inherited something of his love of sport.

Once in Canada I had to get a job. I had sold my car, a Standard 8 Convertible, in England and had £350 as a buffer, which was quite a lot of money in those days, but I needed to work. I wanted to pursue my interest in medicine but initially found employment at a prestigious store, Simpson's, in Toronto. The staff who needed accommodation lived in nearby Fudger House.

I had an introduction to Gordon Gladstone Murray, the first general manager of the Canadian Broadcasting Corporation, who had formerly been with the BBC. Through him I met John Stobo Prichard, who was the extremely distinguished head of neurology at the Hospital for Sick Children in Toronto and my passion for medicine was at last able to be put to use. It had always fascinated me. My connections with the veterinary world had taught me a lot about treating animals and so I knew about anatomy. A friend used to work at the Maudsley Hospital in London and let me watch operations there. I acquired quite a wide knowledge of medicine and assumed I would make a career out of it.

John had joined the neurology staff at the Hospital for Sick Children in Ontario in 1951 to establish an electroencephalography (EEG) laboratory, and was appointed head of the new Division of Neurology. During his 13-year tenure as division head he made lasting contributions to paediatric neurology, particularly in the study and treatment of epilepsy in children. He also established the Child Development Clinic, and served as an adviser to the Ontario government. He offered to train me in administering EEGs and I studied at various hospitals, including the Chapel Hill University hospital in North Carolina, the Presbyterian Hospital in New York and the Montreal general hospital, going on courses and attending lectures. I subsequently took an exam in the subject and was only the fourth person to do it. My certificate, of which I was incredibly proud, is now in the museum at the Hospital for Sick Children.

It was obviously sometimes quite sad working with ill children although, as I generally saw them only for EEGs, I didn't tend to become too involved with them. But there was one little girl of whom I grew particularly fond and it was heart-breaking to have to tell her parents she had an inoperable tumour.

In my work I had to attach electrodes to the patient's head using a sticky paste, called Bentonite. The machines in the early days had valves inside them and, being practical,

I used to maintain and mend them. We had different programmes where we could examine the brain in stages. We could start a seizure in a patient to enable us to see what was wrong. Later we used needles which could be put directly on to the brain. I did biopsies and autopsies and have half a pickled brain to this day as a souvenir! I also edited a relevant journal called *Spike and Wave* that came out several times a year and I would commission articles for it and write pieces myself.

I was permanently on call and never said no. Eventually I trained a couple of girls in the procedures so that I could get a break. John helped to devise an amazing sleeping pill, called Dalmane, which allowed you to wake straight up and get to work without feeling woozy. It was initially created for astronauts so they could leap into action when necessary; it enabled me to sleep during the day when I was on nights and to be alert immediately if the hospital needed me. I still use it now when necessary.

I had to spend some time training in a psychiatric hospital as part of my work and we had to carry lots of keys around for security reasons, to lock some people in and others out. I did some moonlighting to earn extra money at the Jewish Mount Sinai hospital but was eventually told that it wasn't done to have a second job so I had to leave, although I continued to maintain the EEG machines there.

I loved my work and I was extremely diligent and conscientious but I had a great deal of fun, too. I saved up to buy the first car I owned in Canada, an MG TD. Then I got the XK140. I loved that car and took it all over America and Canada when I was on leave. I eventually went to live with the Prichards and had the most wonderful time as they were great lovers of the outdoors, which suited me perfectly.

John's wife Joan was an amazing lady and a wonderful cook and I would help her with the many dinner parties she organised. She had started Meals on Wheels in England and was awarded a CBE for it. Her father, Sir Robert Webber, owned *The Western Mail* newspaper in Cardiff and her mother was the first female judge in Wales. I helped out with the children, Jane, Robert and Sarah, who all became distinguished figures in their respective chosen professions, education, law and medicine, in Canada. I was known as Didi by them – Sarah couldn't say Diana. Robert was a demon when small and used to clash with Joan. She would say: "Didi, *please* go and sort Robert out!" I used to pile all the children into my MG and take them to Sand Lake, which you wouldn't *dream* of doing now, of course, without a seatbelt for each child.

John and Joan owned a huge part of the lake, in North Ontario. The family and I built a log cabin there along with the owner of a local store owner, Geoff Higgins, who was a real craftsman; it was amazing – beautifully constructed and certainly not a shack. We dug the cesspit ourselves and slept in one room, with a single loo. We could get to it only by horse and trailer and had to transport everything we needed that way, too. In the winter we used a sledge. When the lake froze over we walked across from Higgins Point, where Mr Higgins had his store.

We would all canoe while we were at the lake – John taught me expertly – but Joan wasn't keen, so John and I built a dinghy for her in the basement of their house in Toronto. He used to soak the timbers in steaming water in the bath, which didn't please Joan too much! The only problem was that, once built, we couldn't get the dinghy out of the door so we had to take a window out. John later bought Lake Loon, where there were wonderful birds, named loons, which were similar to seagulls and had the most haunting cry. We would canoe there, too, and John taught us all to make fires using just sticks. It all amounted to the most wonderful experience and remains a very important and memorable part of my life.

We would often go skiing and I went to Barrie with staff from the hospital, where we shared a tiny log cabin. I raced and skied for the hospital and John was very pleased that I increased its prestige in this way! He and I and some other doctors attended a medical convention in Montreal and had a marvellous time skiing in the Laurentian mountains.

I had a few boyfriends in Canada, notably Ian Gladstone Murray, who was extremely wealthy and took me to some very sophisticated bars and restaurants and introduced me to his influential friends. Then I met Rolly Allsop, who had a beautiful yacht called The Dawning. He belonged to the Royal Yacht Club on Toronto Island and I would crew for him with some other friends. He was an excellent skipper and I was known as his "first mate"; I still have a treasured mug decorated with the name of his yacht to commemorate the fact. There was an annual race to be first across Lake Ontario when the ice broke in the spring – we usually won it. The Dawning was a large yacht and we all helped to ensure it was prepared thoroughly before taking part, sleeping on board.

I travelled as much as possible at that time. I was determined to see every province of Canada and every state of America – and, to my great satisfaction, I did. I used up all my leave travelling around. I had a good friend, Sandra Malone, whose father was a Morris distributor in Ontario and he lent us a car to do a trip. We drove to Alberta, right across Canada to Lake Louise, Banff, and Vancouver Island. It was very much like England; I loved that. We sometimes slept in the car to save money and took plenty of spares in case of breakdown – I did have to repair the petrol pump at one stage.

We didn't go to camp sites; there weren't that many of them. One night we were in our tent somewhere in the wilds, fairly near the prairies, when suddenly a man appeared. Sandra was very beautiful and he said he was going to make love to her, or words to that effect. I was asleep but I heard Sandra call: "*Di!*" I had a 16-bore shotgun that I kept next to me in the tent. I told the man: "If you get anywhere near my friend I'll shoot you." He more or less jeered at me and said that women couldn't shoot, so I fired a shot at the ground and he took to his heels! Sandra was very shaken but I told her not to worry, I had more cartridges and if he came back I would shoot him, but we didn't see him again. I wasn't really scared. I've never been a scared sort of person.

I was actually a good shot as my step-father, Proby, had taught me to handle a gun in England: I had to learn to beat first, then shoot. I went on a course near Hendon, where they did clay-pigeon shooting. In Canada we went shooting at Sand Lake and I used John's hammer gun, which was difficult to load, before I got my own. On one occasion a doctor who was with us shot a duck and it fell into the lake. It was so cold even the dog refused to retrieve it. John said: "Go on, Didi, you can go and get it," so I stripped to my bra and knickers and went into the icy water after it. The doctor then took the duck home. When Joan heard about it, she said he could at least have given it to me for my trouble! She would have cooked it beautifully.

I went on another road trip in Canada with a boyfriend, John Parish. He was very glamorous but he knew it. I was, too, but I didn't flaunt it like he did! He didn't have much money so I had to pay for most things and he didn't drive my car very well either – I remember feeling quite miffed about it all.

During this time I also visited my uncle, Schubert Smith, who, following his posting as US Consul to Munich after the war, was by then high up in the United States government. He lived in some splendour in Washington with my aunt Gilly. She was an extremely glamorous figure, auburn haired and a bit of an actress.

In Washington, my uncle and aunt had a grand house in a secluded part of the city, set in an acre of grounds. There were about six bedrooms and the hand towels for guests were embroidered with my aunt's initials. There were large lawns and a big driveway up to the house. I remember my uncle being very cross with me because I parked my beloved XK140 on the grass but it had a sump heater and I needed to plug it into a socket in the scullery so that I could start the engine easily, as it was so cold in Washington.

Aunt Gilly gave the most wonderful, formal dinner parties. They were mostly black-tie occasions and the tables were laid with beautiful lace place mats and glittered with cut glass. She had a maid but embassy staff were brought in for bigger events. During my visit President Kennedy was invited to dinner. I was so excited. Unfortunately Jackie, his wife, didn't come, which was a great shame as I was really looking forward to seeing such a stylish and iconic figure.

I remember I wore a cocktail dress with long sleeves, which was the dress code in those days – my aunt would have insisted I did so. Two other friends of my uncle were there and we ate smoked salmon and one of my aunt's superb casseroles, followed by cheese. JFK was the most charming man and much better-looking than his photographs – no wonder all the girls fell for him. He was extremely nice to me but I think he was more interested in my XK140! He was very amusing and a great raconteur. He came with two security men, who ate in the kitchen. He and my uncle got on extremely well and there was a code for when he rang the house, as security had to be tight.

My uncle and aunt used to dine at The White House with the Kennedys. I still treasure a signed photograph of the President that he gave to them and I was appalled when I heard he had been assassinated.

Another friend of my uncle's was Stan Hiller, who founded Hiller helicopters. He also had an XK140 and we got on extremely well. He took me up in his personal helicopter. It was a two-seater and very different from those today.

It was while I was in Canada that my passion for planes really took off. I had always been fascinated by flying, inspired by my father and Aunt Paddy, and so I decided to take some lessons. Central Airways flying school on Toronto Island, run by the Wong brothers, both of whom were excellent instructors, was rated very highly and I decided to go there. I used to catch the ferry over after work.

I can't remember how much the lessons cost but they were much cheaper than in Britain. My instructor was called George Moorwood and I was to fly a Cessna 150, which is a very nice plane. However, my father, who was around at the time, insisted on taking it up first, to check it out. Off he went, to my great embarrassment, and put it through its paces, executing off-the-clock turns, incipient spins and stalls. I remember thinking: "Oh, for goodness sake, don't 'loop' it", as it was not aerobatic! When he landed, he said: "Very sound, nice little plane. My daughter, I am sure, will get on well, thank you."

There was a lot of ground work before I could actually take off. I was taken round the aircraft and told how all the controls worked. Then I was shown the cockpit and George explained all about air speed and pressure. I couldn't wait to get my hands on the controls but George was very strict and we had to take things one step at a time. It seemed ages before I was allowed to have a go myself but it was probably just as well because I remember my first turn was too steep and George had to take over.

Flying from the island was incredible. The lake was beautiful and the shoreline fascinating. My cross-country route was to Hamilton, a pleasant little airfield and very friendly. The Wong brothers also had a 150 seaplane. I went up in it and it was amazing; it took for ever to get airborne but as the lake was so large it wasn't a problem.

While I was in Canada I came home every other year and would save up my leave and the money for my fare; I would usually sail one way and fly back. I was there for about seven years and had decided to stay for longer when I was asked by Toronto University to teach a course on EEGs. The salary was good, I was promised a beautiful duplex on the campus and so I signed a three-year contract. The interview was gruelling but John told me: "Didi, you can do it!"

I then came back to England for a break and to sort out some financial affairs. As it turned out, my last flight trip in Canada was to pilot the 150 to Malton International airport with George. The Prichards took my luggage down for me and I then took the jet back to England. In those days you could visit the cockpit which, of course, I did. The captain and co-pilots were laughing and said to me: "So you were the young lady who flew the 150!" They thought it was very amusing; not many people tended to land a small plane at a large airport. I had a great flight back and still have a picture of my Central Airways log book.

I stayed with Aunt Mim in London, and caught up with friends and had some fun. One day my friend, Joey Holden, whom I had met in Canada and who had worked as an occupational therapist there, decided to organise a trip to Silverstone with a group of friends. Aunt Mim drove me to meet up with them all in Hyde Park. Among the group was a man called Chris Freeman, who captivated me…

Chris was the youngest captain in the Royal Tank Regiment. He had been educated at Tonbridge School but was often in trouble. Once, when the school upset the boys by modernising some of their favourite songs, he changed the tubes in the organ in the chapel around so that when it was next played it created the most dreadful cacophony. He was handsome, lots of fun and we had a great deal in common, particularly a passion for cars and racing. He and his brother, John, had bought an Aston Martin that had originally belonged to Jock Horsfall, who had won Le Mans in it in 1948; Chris subsequently got the fastest lap in it at Brands Hatch.

Chris and I had a whirlwind romance and were married after six months. I thought the fact that I had signed a contract in Canada would be a problem but there was a clause in the small print that provided a let-out. I had to present a letter to the university saying that I planned to marry. Although we were very sorry to part company, John and Joan were pleased for me and did all they could to help.

And so I returned to Canada, packed up my XK140 with my belongings and drove it down to New York. I could hardly bear to watch as my beloved car was swung by crane on to the Queen Mary, prior to the trip back across the Atlantic to Southampton. Chris met me from the ship – and we drove off to begin the next chapter of my life.

My great uncle James Naismith who invented basketball in Canada

My uncle Schubert was a confidant of President Kennedy. I sat next to the world's most glamorous man at dinner in Washington

*My stepmother Helen and Daddy on my half sister
Vivian's graduation day*

The amazing log cabin I helped build at Sand Lake when I was living with the Prichards

My flying badge from
Central Airways in Canada

My Central Airways
log book

In my flying gear when I was learning to be a pilot in Canada

Ensuring everything was shipshape aboard Rolly Allsop's beautiful yacht, The Dawning

Headcorn: Farm and Family

Chris and I were married in St John's Wood on February 28, 1958 and had a reception at 55 Park Lane for 120 guests. My step-father gave me away as my father was in Canada and perhaps didn't feel comfortable attending the wedding with my mother and her new husband there. Daddy told me I could have a lavish wedding but if I opted for a smaller one he would give me the latest electrical goods: an English Electric fridge, a twin-tub and a dishwasher – I opted for the latter.

My beautiful dress came from Harrods and I had to have it taken in – I had a marvellous figure in those days! It had a small train and I wore a little coronet with pearls. My half-sister, Lorna, was my bridesmaid and my eight-year-old cousin, Patrick Quirk, was my page. In later years he became a sound and lighting engineer for the BBC; my aunt Julie, who adored him, left him her house in Cadogan Lane.

Chris had been stationed in Bovington and used to operate in Hobart's Funnies, modified tanks that played a major part during the invasion of Normandy. We spent our honeymoon in a local pub in Bovington. I had a Dior suit to go away in and climbed in and out of the tanks in it when Chris showed me round! My mother bought me a beautiful negligee for my wedding night – but, unfortunately, Chris met his old sergeant in the bar and refused to come to bed, to my great annoyance!

Chris's family owned Shenley Farm at Headcorn in Kent, which had a farm manager. The property had been a satellite for West Malling airfield during the Second World War, used by the American, Canadian, and Polish airforces, as well as our own, and in those days was known as Lashenden. (Flying ace Johnnie Johnson later unveiled a plaque at the airfield's museum to commemorate its significance.) There was a permanent military presence on the farm during the war and even the family had to have passes to get to it. When the military planes landed or took off the lane that went past what became our family home was shut as the runway went straight across it. The airfield was still used very occasionally but when Chris and I moved to the farm there was very little movement.

There were several properties on the farm and, after our marriage, we chose to make our home in a 16th-century cottage, known as White House Cottage. It was virtually in ruins and initially we slept in one room on a sofa-bed but we gradually made it habitable, did it up and extended it. When our second child, Elizabeth, was born we added on more rooms and eventually it comprised seven bedrooms and three bathrooms. I spent a lot of my own money on it: I had a dining room built around the huge table that came from The Firs, which could seat 16. Chris and I built a small side extension ourselves – we even did the bricklaying!

We had lovely parties and I had a special floor installed in the dining room for dancing – a removable carpet was put over the top. Because I was so keen on good wine, and had grown up with it at The Firs, I had a special wine store installed off the dining room. The stairs were reinforced and a stone floor was put in to keep the bottles cool. I designed a fireplace with exquisite biblical tiles, which are worth a fortune now. We did have a good lifestyle, but I also worked hard on the farm and did most of the books.

I loved running the 300-acre estate and helped build it up – I knew more about it than Chris did. He initially worked in the family poultry business at Smithfield, J. J. Freeman and Sons, with his brother, John, but then grew more interested in farming. My veterinary knowledge was a great help with the animals and I could give them injections, diagnose their illnesses and generally look after their health and welfare. We kept pigs and I did a lot of the practical work involved. We bought in weaners to fatten up and had the largest heavy hog contract with Wall's, taking them up to the company's premises in London in a two-tier Bedford lorry.

There were also 600 sheep on the farm. We lambed outside and took it in turns to do the night shift, dozing in a sleeping bag in a lovely old shepherd's hut. I had a pony called Jango and he was as good as a dog for rounding up the sheep. If I needed to transport a sick ewe back to the farm I would put it across his saddle.

We had a house cow called Clarabelle. I used to milk her but if I was late for any reason the farm staff would nip in and do it and help themselves to her milk – they thought it was a great joke! One farm hand, old Arthur Saunders, used to say: "You can 'ave a bit 'o mine then!"

When Chris and I married the hop pickers who used to come down to the farm every year from London gave us a beautiful china tea set as a wedding present, which is still at Headcorn. Hop growing was one of the most fascinating areas of life on the farm. We had 12 acres and an oast house where Chris used to do the drying at night. We used the umbrella method of stringing and a stringer on stilts would set it all up. I could never do it – it was a real art form.

The hop pickers would arrive towards the end of the summer and we would collect them from Headcorn Station in a tractor and trailer. There was a row of hoppers' huts on the farm which all had bunk beds and the families would return to the same ones every year. They could decorate them as they liked and some of the wallpaper chosen was quite extraordinary, all topped off with little lace curtains! The hoppers were often great characters and became our friends. "Lil" was a particular favourite. She loved Jamie and Elizabeth and kept her hut on long after we gave up the hops.

The hops were gathered in and the bines were laid across special bins that were hung on tripods and then the hoppers would strip them – the children all had to do their bit as well. The hops were put into baskets with two handles and we measured them and paid the hoppers accordingly. Each hopper had a number and the amount he or she picked was entered next to it on a chart. Mr Abbott, who helped do the farm books, would sort it out. I used to go to the bank in Headcorn to fetch their wages – occasionally they asked for a sub!

The hops were packed into hop sacks, known as pockets, and we were paid according to the quality. We had to meet certain quotas and dealt with a hop factor, or agent. Ours was Dudley Le May, who was also a trustee of Tonbridge School and very charming. He would invite us to grand occasions connected with the industry in the City, where hop samples were judged according to the quality. We were then traditionally treated to Stilton cheese and port.

We loved the hops and the hopping. We used to string some of the bines around the kitchen and delighted in the smell of them. The hoppers had wonderful knees-ups and sing-songs – sometimes we would go along. We always gave a party for them when hopping came to an end for another year. As time went on and people generally became more affluent they started to arrive in their cars – they were often smarter than ours. One day one of the farm hands heard a hopper say to another: "Hey, you'd better move your car. The Guv [Chris] is coming on his bike and he parks there!" We heard that later one chap ended up with a Rolls-Royce! It was so sad when the industry declined and we had to sell our quota. A precious piece of Kentish history was lost and we felt it keenly.

While staying on the farm the hoppers' children were always warned that, with all the machinery and other hazards, it could be a dangerous place – they were forbidden to go near the River Beult, which flowed for a mile through our land. Fortunately none of them came to grief, but Jamie almost did. When he was small he had one of the first Puffa-style down jackets that I got from Canada. It was blue and yellow. We had a cesspit that contained the slurry from the pigs and Jamie liked to jump up and down on a piece of tin that had been placed across it. One day he fell in – it was 12 feet deep! Fortunately, his jacket kept him afloat and Chris and old Arthur, who was in charge of the pigs, managed to fish him out. He remembers being hosed down with icy water before I took him home and put him in a hot bath.

When Jamie was a baby I used to push his pram down to old Arthur and he would look after him for a while. One day I had prepared a bottle of milk for Jamie and he threw it right into the pig bodge, which was full of swill ready to be served up. Arthur, being a practical sort of fellow, picked it up with a dollop of swill on it, wiped the teat on his less than pristine overalls and popped it straight back into Jamie's mouth. I'm glad to say that he survived that, too!

We rotated crops and grew a lot of wheat on the farm, using an old combine-harvester and storing it in silos. The wheat came down a chute, was bagged up, put on to the tractor and trailer and sent off to the silos. I was strong and played a big part, lifting the 1 cwt sacks. I also used to plough when necessary. You then had to disc the land – that gave you better tilth – then harrow it and roll it and put the seed in. (When my daughter, Elizabeth, was overdue Chris sent me to do some discing, about 50 acres, in the hope that it would hurry things along, but it didn't work!)

Chris and I worked hard but we had a lot of fun. He loved to drive my XK140 in the early days and used to take it up to Smithfield market. One day, on his way home, he had a crash. It wasn't his fault – someone drove into him but, fortunately, as the car was left-hand drive and it was the front offside that was hit, he escaped unharmed. On a lighter note, he had some game with him and one of the farm hands delighted in telling me that "the Governor had had two birds in the back"! I later had the car rebuilt and turned into right-hand drive.

When I was pregnant with Jamie my waters broke early but Chris told me to go back to sleep, the baby wasn't due for three weeks! However, as my pains grew really bad, our GP, Dr Hardwick, told him to get me up to the London Clinic, where I was booked in. Chris put the front seat back, grabbed towels and a bottle of brandy and drove at over 100 mph all the way. He was longing to be stopped by the police so he could say his wife was having a baby but he wasn't spotted, even when he went through red lights! I had a bad time delivering Jamie and had to have 47 stitches – I should have had a Caesarean. At home once more I had two wonderful girls to help me – Flora McDonald first of all and then Frances John. Frances came from a farming family and went on to become wealthy in her own right, owning farms in Australia and New Zealand, I believe. She met her husband at our farm.

My mother got on very well with Chris – he called her "Mummy"! She adored Jamie, who christened her "Grammoo", and looked after him whenever she could. She bought two cots, one for us and one for when he stayed at her home in Hampstead. Sadly, she didn't live long enough to see him grow up – she died in 1963, when he was three. Mummy had complained of backache but I felt there was something more serious wrong with her. She went for investigations at the London Clinic and it was thought that she had cancer of the oesophagus. But the surgeons found that the cancer had spread to every single organ; there was nothing they could do for her and gave her three months to live.

I was pregnant with Elizabeth at the time and it was so sad. Mummy was divorced from my stepfather by then, so Lorna looked after her, aided by a nurse, and I helped as much as possible. I didn't tell her I was pregnant because I was having to lift her and I didn't want to worry her. I was quite sick though and she said: "Diana, why do you *keep* going to the loo?" I often did the nights, sleeping on a mattress on the floor. She was cremated at Golders Green – I didn't go to the service, as women still didn't tend to go to funerals, but I organised the wake at her house. I saw Daddy shortly before he died, aged 92 in 1996, in America – I was heartbroken to lose them both.

My wedding day. I was so excited to be Chris's bride; we had so much in common

One of the last pictures of me and my dear Daddy. He died in 1996

Headcorn: Taking Off

Although I was fully wrapped up in farming and my young family I still hankered after flying. I had money from my grandfather's trust and had also saved while I was in Canada. I eventually decided to buy a plane of my own. I chose an Auster 5 (GAJGJ), which had been rebuilt by the Allen brothers, who were engineers. They had flown into Headcorn in a little Turbulent plane and we got to know them. The Auster had three seats and was semi-aerobatic with a Sutton harness and cost £7,000. My friend Neville Browning, the famous aerobatic pilot, gave it the once-over and said he couldn't fault it.

I kept it at Rochester airport first of all, but it got "hangar rash", ie people kept bumping other planes into it, so we decided to build a hangar at Headcorn – we had plenty of room. We bought the shell from Newport Pagnell. Chris and I collected it on a flatbed Bedford lorry and took it home and unloaded it with the help of an old crane that we called Nellie – its tracks didn't work and we had to pull it around with a tractor. We had the Auster in one end of the hangar and sheep in the other, with straw bales in between. With Health and Safety you wouldn't be allowed to do that now!

I could taxi the Auster right into the hangar – you're not supposed to do that, it can be terribly dangerous. The propellers had to be swung round to start it – it was quite an art. I could do it myself when I was preparing to fly off somewhere but "young" Alf who worked on the farm was fantastic at it and so was Chris. Initially three turns were made with the ignition off, then you sucked in or primed it. I would set the throttle and turn the ignition on before the propellers were swung again. Whoever was swinging had to put their hands on the top and yell to everyone to keep clear. We would both then give an "OK" signal and the person who was swinging the propellers would push downwards. It was vital to ensure that no clothing was flapping loose; a tie caught in the propeller, for instance, could be fatal.

Once the engine was going I'd put my thumbs up to indicate I was ready to go. I had my own chocks made for me; they were yellow with red lettering with my initials and the Auster's registration. I was rather proud of them and took them everywhere with me – when we had more aircraft no one would dare touch them! I did start the plane on my own sometimes; that would have been frowned upon, but I made sure the brakes were on and the chocks were under.

When I started to fly I used to land and take off in nearby fields, using part of the old runway which was grass. During the war metal tracking had been laid along the runway which was necessary to support the heavy military aircraft that used it. That had been taken up and we used it for fencing around the farm. When more people began flying into Headcorn Chris extended the runway area and drained it to make it more usable.

I had been buzzing happily around in the Auster for about three months before I learnt, to my dismay, that my licence wasn't legal in England. An instructor at Rochester airport pointed it out when he said my log book needed signing – and then found it was Canadian and not valid in Britain. I had studied air law and navigation in Canada but it was under Canadian air law and navigation rules. I then had to study for my British licence but fortunately, Neville Browning, who was also a chief flying instructor, stepped in to help.

I flew up to up to Stapleford Tawney, where Neville lived, but another pilot had to accompany me to as I was no longer allowed to fly on my own; it was really ridiculous as I had so much experience. The airfield there had a fleet of Ercoupes, a very easy aeroplane to fly, and I got my licence in one of those.

I had to do a General Flight Test, a long cross-country and a short cross-country trip. The long cross-country was from Stapleford Tawney to Ipswich, Ipswich to Rochester and Rochester to Stapleford Tawney. The short one was from Stapleford Tawney to Rochester. I also had to do a written air test and the whole thing took about four days.

Neville was the most amazing pilot, unbelievably talented. He used to fly an aerobatic plane called a Zlin and I have a picture of him upside down in it on which he wrote: "To Diana, Happy memories... With love, Neville." He was an older man and extremely handsome and debonair – he always smoked Gauloises – and I stayed with him and his wife while I was qualifying for my certificate. I loved his greyhounds and he became very fond of my little Jack Russell, Hoppy, so I used to fly him up to Essex with me. Apparently not many pilots take their dogs up with them!

Neville taught me to do aerobatics. You had to do "incipient" spins in those days; I don't think you have to do them now. This involved doing a half-spin and then straightening up, but he said: "Oh well, Di, I think it's better we do the whole spin." We went up to 6,000 feet... I managed to acquit myself! As the Auster was only semi-aerobatic I couldn't do inverted flying in it, only spins and loops. The first time Neville did an inverted circuit with me on board I was terrified and closed my eyes.

When I had to do my long cross-country trip there was a hell of a tail wind coming back. I didn't work it all out properly and realised I had overshot Stapleford Tawney, so I had to turn round and go back. However, it was all worth it when I received my British licence and was free to fly again.

As an engineer Chris was very interested in planes and eventually I taught him to fly. He became an excellent pilot and navigator – funnily enough, we never had a row when I was teaching him! I was always No. 1, in the left-hand seat. He did what I told him and I could over-ride him. He learnt very quickly and his co-ordination was amazing but, despite his skill, he never did bother to get his licence. As Headcorn didn't have a licence to instruct at that time he couldn't go solo there but he went to Lympne, did one circuit, and they sent him up alone. He flew the Auster, and the Dauphin that we later purchased, perfectly when I was with him.

When we expanded Headcorn Chris used to do the Radio Traffic Control, working in an old caravan. He was excellent at that: he knew the area so well and was very kind and helpful, and could talk people back to our airfield if they were lost. (I still have my first Bakelite navigation equipment. In those days you worked everything out with a slide rule and had to know all about air speed, ground speed and wind.)

I taught my children to fly, too. Initially I did a short circuit with them to see how they felt; I didn't want them to be sick. Jamie could fly at eight years old. He was brilliant, a natural but, as he was so young, I remember having to prop him up with cushions so that he could see properly. We would go up to 2,000 feet and he would take over and do some gentle turns. He always wanted to do a little bit more, ie steeper turns, and I would have to say: "Level up, please!", but he was very capable even then and I was quite confident in him. Elizabeth became very competent, too, and eventually got her licence in America.

Jamie remembers flying with me up to Norfolk to pick up some chicken vaccine for us and other local farmers. When we came in to land the runway on the farm was too short and piled up with rubble, so we ended up spinning round on to the grass; a bit scary but he was pretty sanguine about it.

The children were quite blasé about our unusual lifestyle. They only ever travelled by car or by plane but one day they said: "Why can't we go on a bus or a train, like *other* people?" When we were next at what was then our holiday home, the old coastguard cottage at Pett Level, in East Sussex, where Robin and I now live, I decided to take them into Hastings on the little local bus. The first shock came when it suddenly veered off the route I thought we would take and started going all over Fairlight – I wondered where we could possibly be going.

Once in Hastings we did loads of shopping and then I said to the children: "Now, where did Mummy leave the car?" They chorused: "Don't be silly Mummy, we're on the *bus*!" I had no idea where the bus went back from and once we had found it, we had to drag all the shopping on to it. I don't know what on earth the other passengers made of us. Then Elizabeth piped up helpfully: "Mummy never normally takes the bus, you see," which probably made things worse! After that, they didn't want to go on a bus again…

One year we were flying to Austria on a skiing trip in a 727. I, of course, wanted to see in the cockpit and the pilot allowed me to sit at the controls. I told him about my flying experience and that I had flown nothing larger than a twin but he said that I could "have a go"! I did a gentle turn, which obviously alarmed some of the passengers. Elizabeth did nothing to calm their fears by telling everyone in the cabin: "It's all right. Mummy's flying it!"

At Headcorn the word spread that the old wartime runway was in use once more and people started wanting to fly in. It was half a mile long – I could land the Auster within 350 yards – but we increased it bit by bit and today it is even longer. We were only allowed to have so many "movements" and were "prior permission" only at first but the Army Air Corps gave us our first movement book to record all the landings and that enabled us, in 1969, to get one of the first existing users certificates. Chris did all the hard work involved in that. We ended up having pilots to stay overnight at the farm and I used to give them breakfast. The Air Registration Board representative came down to check the engineering work we did on the planes at the airfield. He would bring his wife and stay the night.

As we expanded we got into *Pooley's Flight Guide* (the airfield's frequency is 122.000). Headcorn was really on the map then. We used to charge five shillings for landing fees, about 25p now. The sheep had to be moved out of the hangar as more people wanted to use it to house planes overnight. Chris built on to it and eventually some aircraft were kept there permanently. We didn't charge landing fees if the planes were kept with us, which was unusual.

The calves were kept in a wooden building on the farm. Chris partitioned it off and set up the RT at one end. I also began a small canteen in there. I had been catering in the house but it became increasingly difficult to provide for the increasing numbers. A Calor gas stove and a sink were sited in the corner of the shed and we bought provisions at the "cash and bash it", as we called it. I had some enormous frying pans and would serve up "Flying Breakfasts" – eggs, bacon, sausages and toast – and people would fly in especially for them. Many pilots were our friends and I always seemed to be cooking for masses of people.

The Army Air Corps used to visit to practise 'waltzing' in a group of helicopters at Headcorn for the displays that they gave all over Britain and Europe. They would often stay overnight – I think they liked my cooking. I was intrigued by their routines and their skills and, in the end, they allowed me to go up with them. It was against the rules and so I had to put on one of their uniforms in case I was spotted!

When people we knew dropped into Headcorn they often clamoured for a "ride". These little trips were usually incident free and pleasurable but one wasn't. I took one chap up and once we were airborne he panicked and grabbed the dual control stick on his side. It was a dangerous situation. I shouted at him to let go and eventually hit him across the face with one hand while hanging on to my stick with the other. I was about to clout him again when he calmed down a bit.

When I got back down Chris said: "What the hell were you doing?" I told him in no uncertain terms that there would be no more "joy rides" unless we knew exactly the type of person we were taking up. Chris then said that it was possible to unscrew the second stick and take it out of the plane; that was what we would do in future to save me from having to bash anyone else!

I've always been very keen on photography and own several cameras. If I needed to take aerial photographs at Headcorn for any reason I would just lift the door off the Auster and fly without it, so that the structure didn't get in the way of the lens. It was quite safe as I was strapped in. However, removing the plane door also came in useful on other occasions. Chris had a particularly large aunt and the only way I could get her on board was to remove the door and then replace it once she was securely in her seat!

At one stage we decided to try to cater for night flying and I went to Biggin Hill to get my night rating. We did some trials on landing lights and this proved to be quite a frightening experience for me. I went up in the Dauphin at dusk and Chris put out some reflector lights – they were attached to upside-down triangles either side of the runway – but the plane's lights didn't pick them up well enough and I couldn't see them, or where to land. I did four overpasses and began to worry that I would run out of fuel, although I always kept the tank topped up.

I eventually called Chris to ask the farm staff to get the tractor out with its lights full blaze and also to put the creamery lights on, which were very powerful, so that I could see my way in. But even with all those I couldn't judge the height properly. I went round and round I don't know how many times before I managed to get down. I was quite shaken – it certainly wasn't an experience I would want to repeat. Chris wasn't too concerned. He said: "I knew you'd do it." We scrapped the reflectors after that and replaced them with paraffin goose-neck flares which worked very well. Now Headcorn has excellent lighting and people can get their night ratings there.

Unfortunately, as the aerodrome expanded the locals were up in arms. Chris was very good at deflecting their attacks. His first question was always: "When did you move to the area?" If the answer was "last year", he would say: "Well, why on earth buy a house near an airfield?" However, we never flew over the village itself, always across the surrounding countryside, and there are now restrictions regarding the circuit you can use.

Although I had only really envisaged being able to fly my plane and to have other pilots drop in, Chris was keen for the whole operation to grow even more. He started to do more engineering work on planes and the company began gradually to expand.

I had no idea then that my "fun" project would evolve into the "empire" it is today, or of the excitement, adventures – and problems – that it would bring with it.

My picture of Shenley Farm – I flew with the doors off the Auster for a clearer view

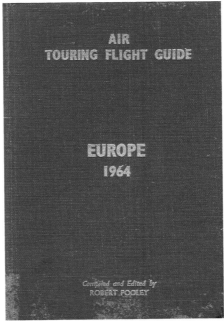

Pooley's Guide became my bible when I was flying in Europe

Showing them the ropes - I taught both my children to fly and they became first-class pilots, Jamie eventually taking over Headcorn. **Daily Mirror**

Jamie's first lesson. He was only eight and had to be propped up with cushions

Headcorn: Flying High

I did a great deal of flying and made many friends in the aviation world. My friend and mentor, Neville Browning, frequently performed at air shows all over Britain and in Europe and, later on, I used to go with him. Because I was experienced in aircraft maintenance he trusted me to do the pre-flight inspections to ensure that his Zlin was airworthy and safe: it is vital to be extremely methodical and examine virtually every inch of the plane, checking that everything is in place and that the fuel doesn't have any water in it.

I had learnt a fair amount about maintenance in Canada but when I got my own plane I wanted to know more about looking after it. The Auster had a Lycoming engine and Chris and I were able to do most of the maintenance ourselves. We had an engineer on the farm who checked our work out as the ARB was extremely strict – quite rightly so – and awarded Certificates of Airworthiness only to planes that were in first-class working order.

When I travelled to shows with Neville, he would go off to talk to the organisers at the show about what he planned to do and I would look after the Zlin. He trusted me totally and we developed a great affection for each other. He was gallant, a real gentlemen. I think he might have been a bit of a ladies' man, but I didn't see that side of him. I really admired him, but more for his flying than for anything else.

The only time I recall Neville making any error of judgment was at a show in Belgium, attended by the country's king and queen. As always, I checked his Zlin thoroughly before he went up. I never left it. He put on a faultless display but when it ended he came in very low and failed to put the undercarriage down. I thought the Zlin might catch fire but Neville was such a fantastic pilot, somehow he managed to land without disastrous consequences. However, he was extremely upset and embarrassed – the Zlin was his "skin" and he was meticulous in caring for it and checking it over. The undercarriage would have been inspected by both of us – you lie underneath the plane on your back to do it.

Neville was so down that he didn't want to be presented to the royal couple but in the end he was persuaded to go through with it. Everybody cheered him, although no one could understand what had gone wrong and neither could he. Presumably he simply forgot to put the undercarriage down.

I had to hitch a lift back to England. It was Elizabeth's half-term and I was determined not to miss it. I got a ride in a five-seater – there were six of us, so it was a bit worrying and not very comfortable, but at least I got home. Fortunately the ladies on board didn't weigh very much but we didn't have enough seat belts. It wasn't the kind of thing I usually did.

I didn't carry on doing aerobatics but I loved to watch them. We had some top-flight exponents drop in to Headcorn. James Black was one revered pilot who used to come to us to practise. Ray Hanna, the leader of the Red Arrows, was another visitor. Headcorn was popular for this because of its rural setting; pilots have to perform aerobatics over open country by law.

"Pashley" was another wonderful character from the flying world and a favourite of mine. He was a legend who started the air club at Shoreham; it was very much like Headcorn, with two runways. Pashley was an amazing gentleman and we got on very well; he helped me quite a lot and I flew one of the oldest Tiger Moths in the world with him. He was a little man and Vera, his wife, was a tall woman – she said that when he died Shoreham wouldn't be the same without him, so she was going to have him stuffed and put in the corner of the club house! She didn't carry out her promise but there is a room named after him now at the airport.

Another visitor to Headcorn was the distinguished woman pilot Sheila Scott; unfortunately, I annoyed her! Sheila broke more than 100 light-aircraft records between 1965 and 1972 and was the first British pilot to fly solo around the world and the first to fly over the North Pole. She was so relaxed when in the air that she would play tapes to teach herself Spanish while she was flying.

One year there was an air display at Lydd and Sheila and I were both there. The owner, Mick de Wolfson, was a friend of mine and very good to me. Some time earlier I had had to fly into Lydd as it was clamped [fog bound] at Headcorn; I was in a twin-propeller Aztec which we had bought by that time. The landing fees for it were £40 but when Mick realised it was me he cancelled the fees. He had a horse, as I did, and, as a thank you, I bought him a beautiful leather head-collar with his horse's name on it.

At the Lydd air show he asked me to show off my four-seater Dauphin as it was such a beautiful aeroplane. He wanted me to do some slow runs, about 40mph, just on the stall. I said of course! The Red Arrows were coming in and he thought it would be impressive if the Dauphin were to come in really slowly, then the Red Arrows would fly in quite low, but at about 100 times my speed. It all went off perfectly and it was really thrilling to be a part of it. But Sheila was absolutely livid because she wasn't asked to do anything. Then the weather closed in and she asked to stay at Headcorn! She smoked like a chimney [she later died of lung cancer] and I had to tell her to go outside

– I couldn't have smoke in the house because Jamie suffered with asthma. Sheila was furious. It was more or less: "Don't you *realise* who I *am*?" Of course, I was nothing, just a woman with her own plane, a "flying mum", as the press later dubbed me, but *she* was Sheila Scott!

I flew in the annual King's Cup air race in an Aztec D with Eric Gardener, who owned the Gatwick Hotel. The race was established by George V to encourage the development of light aircraft and engine design and the route went across Britain. I was supposed to navigate but the P2, or co-pilot, who was a friend of Eric's, suddenly became ill. Eric rang up one night and said: "Sorry Di, you've got to be P2 *and* you've got to navigate!" A wonderful instructor at Biggin Hill helped me with the navigation – I swotted like mad! Eric was really proud of our efforts and his wife was so sweet and supportive; she bought me a gold charm to mark the occasion – it was a perfect little plane with tiny wheels and a propeller that turned. I still wear it today when I'm flying.

Chris bought the Aztec A when Headcorn started to expand. The insurance was very high and you had to have 20 hours as P1, or first pilot, on a twin before you could fly it, which I managed to do. I clocked up so many flying hours that I was able to give some away – letting pilots trying to get their licences to put themselves down as P1 and me as P2 when we went up together – which was very silly in hindsight. I also bought Chris another Auster with a Cirrus engine which had been damaged and we rebuilt it in the tractor shed together. It took us about six months. I did a lot of work on the airframe and went over to the gliding club at Challock, near Canterbury, to get some guidance, where they were very helpful. Chris rebuilt the engine. This caused some conflict as he became quite obsessed and would spend many hours working on it. He was often late for supper and I would get very cross but, as I had bought it for him, I suppose I had no real grounds for complaint!

I took it for a test flight when the work was completed. Cables run through the structure and if the tension is not correct in the ailerons and the tail the aircraft won't fly properly. I taxied up and down for quite a while before I finally took off and made a note of everything that struck me. Then Chris came with me and we went through an exhaustive checklist. Finally it was all done to our satisfaction and was signed off by a Polish engineer who lived in a cottage by the tractor shed and became part of the team. It seemed like a pretty big achievement and we were delighted. We had a bottle of Champagne to celebrate the fact that we now had His and Her planes!

In those days I used to fly to France to get my fuel on a drawback scheme; it was about half the price. I refuelled at an airfield in Berck-sur-Mer, which belonged to some friends. We'd fly round France and come home. I also did air rallies, one to Deauville. I was very cross on one occasion as there were women there flying helicopters and one got all the accolades. I was in a fixed-wing and no one took any notice of me! I also took part in the Jersey air rally.

These were wonderful, happy years and we had a huge amount of fun. We used to throw massive parties on the farm, sometimes for as many as 200 people who belonged to local organisations such as the Bonfire Society and members of Rochester Flying Club – I would do all the catering myself. The Red Arrows even put on a display at one of our rallies. We had upgraded to a Dauphin, which we both loved; our flying exploits got Chris and me into the news and, out of the blue, I was invited to go on the trip of a lifetime which turned into much more of an adventure than I had bargained for. We also had a beautiful sailing boat and even bought a Bentley! It seemed as if life couldn't get any better…

Media Darling

Chris and I were constantly hopping across the Channel in the plane, on shopping and business trips and to various social events such as the RAF ball at Laarbruch in Germany, and I would fly Chris round the country for business and stock purchasing. Before long I started to become well known for my exploits and attracted the attention of the media. I met someone from the William Hickey gossip column in the Daily Express *at a party held in London by my friends from Pett Level, the Woodroffes. I suppose I was very glamorous in those days with my flowing auburn hair and an adventurous spirit to match. A piece appeared in the* Express *about "the flying housewife" and then it all took off.*

Articles about me flying to Goodwood and taking Chris on business trips appeared in the Daily Sketch, *and the* Daily Mirror *dubbed me "the flying mum". It mentioned visits to friends and shopping by plane. There were pictures of me and the children in the Auster — even Hoppy the Jack Russell got in on the act.*

The Express *did a photo feature on "the flying housewife home from shopping" and showed me coming in to land, scattering the sheep. Chris was quoted as saying the flock were all very "air-minded", and not scared of the plane at all.*

We often appeared in the Kent Messenger, *the* Kent and Sussex Courier, *the* Kentish Express *and* Kent Life *and I was interviewed on* Southern Television. *The* Reader's Digest *quoted me talking about how I would often pop over to France to do the family shopping and there was more in the* Daily Sketch *about these trips. I told them it was cheaper to fly to France than to go by train to London — I shopped there for Chris's favourite foods, which included snails and salami. Jamie and Elizabeth loved to go with me and it certainly helped to improve their French!*

I was asked to publicise the ice rink in Brighton as I was a pretty competent skater and used to visit the rink quite often. I decided to fly into Shoreham airport with Chris, Jamie and Elizabeth, rather than drive to Brighton. The rink sent two cars to pick us up and it caused quite a stir in the local press. It was great publicity for the rink and they were very pleased.

The Sun *did a piece on the increasing number of people who were buying their own planes, after comedian Dick Emery's Tiger Moth damaged a parked car. It quoted Chris talking about the economic benefits. "[Planes]… are absolutely invaluable," he said. "We can go and check up on the sheep in 10 minutes instead of the two hours it would take on foot." He told the paper we did 20 miles to the gallon at 100mph, at the same price a motorist paid for premium grade. "Flying costs me less than if I used a car or public transport – and it's enormously quicker." We were also featured in* Weekend *and* Farmer and Stockbreeder *and I appeared yet again in the* Daily Sketch *when I planned to fly to my cousin's wedding in Portugal. The paper also reported that we had added a hangar to the farm buildings and made quite a thing of our His and Her planes.*

In 1967 the Kent Messenger *had a feature about how we had bought the Dauphin and the fact that I had a trouser suit in the exact colour to match it.*

The Dauphin

We upgraded to the Dauphin (GAVOG), much like another family would a car. It had four seats, which meant we could all travel together and was much faster than the Auster and more fun to fly. We commissioned it from the manufacturers in Dijon and had it modified to include better seats and a special area in the back to store our skis. I wanted two altimeters, which tell you how high you are: one is set at sea level and the other at the barometric pressure. Airports give you their pressure and you set one altimeter to that so you know your exact height when you prepare to land. It was quite advanced for the time. You could get the Dauphin "on the step", changing the plane's angle, and it would go 5mph faster.

I chose the Dauphin's colour scheme myself – tangerine, a safe colour and easily spotted and more or less the same colour as my hair! – and it was eventually adopted by the company as standard. I was so excited I took the company's colour chart to London and eventually, after two days, tracked down a suit in the exact shade in Harrods. I bought another locally, so I had one for summer and one for winter, with skirt, jacket, trousers and matching gloves! It was such fun and I still have bits of my outfits. My sitting-room ceiling is tangerine now, as is the front door of Marigold, another tiny seaside cottage that I owned in Sussex, a few doors from my home, and which has now been given to Jamie.

I had a special lightweight tent made to carry in the Dauphin. It was more than six feet high, so that Chris could stand up in it, and had a floor and awning with an area to cook in. We would often go to Berck and camp on the airfield there; there was a lovely amusement park nearby for the children. We had been introduced to Rene and Yvette Valois, the owners, by Neville. They would listen out for his Zlin to arrive when he was expected as the engine made a very distinctive noise, and would clear the field to allow Neville to do an inverted circuit before landing. When he died the Valoises had a picture of him put up with a black band on it.

The Dauphin also had a VOR navigational aid. I had always flown visual, so this was something new for me to learn. I had to take my Instrument Meteorological Conditions rating (IMC), which was certainly challenging. Once you had learnt about the instruments you were instructed to do a let-down from a beacon and fly with a hood over your head to prove that you knew what you were doing. Then the instrument panel was blacked out. You took the exam with only three instruments to look at – it was quite hard. You had to drop from 2,000 feet to 200 on instruments alone and couldn't look out until you got to 200 feet – there was certainly no peeping allowed. My notes were pages and pages long; I really don't know how I did it.

We did a lot more in the Dauphin. The payload was better and the centre of gravity was different, so it was even better for shopping. One year we all went on a pre-Christmas shopping trip to France and loaded up with all kinds of presents, food and other goodies. The plane was up to its weight limit, the children were squashed into the back and Chris was wedged in the passenger seat. On the way home we had to clear customs at Lydd. The officers asked if we had anything to declare and when I told them that we just had presents and Christmas items they didn't believe me – they demanded that we unload the whole lot! Chris was absolutely furious but we had to ask for a luggage trolley and do what they asked. It was piled up with our things and we knew we would never get everything back in again – in the end we left it all there. Chris told the officers we had to get back to the farm and so we had to return to collect all the stuff the next day in the shooting brake. We didn't really think it was very funny although the customs people did!

We had friends in Dijon and would fly over to them in the Dauphin and then drive up to the Alps from there to go winter skiing. One year we were in Cervinia and saw a man riding a kind of snow mobile. Jamie and Elizabeth urged me to ask if they could have a ride! The driver, who was Italian, said yes, they could. We started chatting about the machine and engines in general and he asked if I was interested in cars. He said he "had Fiats" – he turned out to be the boss of Fiat! I asked him about the range and said I was after something fast. He told me I should go to the Motor Show in England. I did go and went to the Fiat stand, where the staff asked me to help out.

The company was bringing out a new sports model and asked me to use it for a while and write a report. I used to drive it along our local roads but unfortunately got stopped by the police for speeding when I was on my way to Eastbourne – I was doing about 80mph. Fiat had said that if this kind of thing occurred they had an arrangement with the police but I had to activate it within 10 minutes by phoning a certain number. When the police had left I tore off to the nearest garage – we didn't have mobile phones in those days – and begged to use the phone. Thankfully I did manage to get off the hook and didn't have to pay a fine. Fiat then asked me to model with some cars. They brought two to the farm and took pictures of me with the vehicles and a plane, which appeared in the company's house magazine. As a reward I was given free servicing for my car.

When I eventually left Chris I sold the Dauphin as I needed the money but I had been terribly sad to let it go. I sold it to an airline pilot. Before the sale I offered to take him up on a circuit to explain the plane's little eccentricities and other details, such as loading and its centre of gravity, but I got the impression that he decided he didn't need any help from me, a "flying mum"! Sometime afterwards it was involved in an accident on take-off in a field – fortunately no one was hurt. I went with Chris to recover it at the request of the ARB, which *wanted an engineer to examine it and Chris was able to arrange for its transportation. I was heart-broken at the sight of my beautiful, damaged plane and was in tears.*

African Adventure

Patrick Speedy was an Army Air Corps pilot whom we knew quite well. He was very keen to do a month-long trip to South Africa because his brother lived there and he asked if we would go with him: me to help fly and Chris to navigate. Chris felt he couldn't spare the time away from the farm but said it would be all right for me to go along. We were to be away over Christmas 1964, which was a pity as I would miss both Chris and Jamie's birthdays as well as the holiday, but it really was an opportunity not to be ignored. Patrick arranged to borrow a Tri-pacer, which belonged to the Royal Engineers. Space was at a premium – we couldn't really have fitted Chris in. I took one small case and had to think my "wardrobe" through very carefully. I was tremendously worried about having enough underwear and in the end settled for packs of throwaway knickers!

We had to accommodate drinking water in cans, Army rations and biscuits brought by Patrick, sleeping bags, a lightweight tarpaulin for emergencies, and four jerry cans of fuel. We also had to take some steps made at Rochester Flying Club as the filler for the fuel tank was right on the top of the wing. A funnel and a chamois leather to keep any muck out of the fuel were vital.

Patrick and I left on December 18 and were extremely lucky with the weather. I don't remember being held up at all. We cleared customs at Lympne and set off for Le Touquet, where we also dealt with customs. We worked out the fuel and did "hops" down the length of France, stopping in places such as Berck, Toulouse and Macon, and got as far as Nice before crossing to Ajaccio on Corsica and then Cagliari on Sardinia. I did a running map as I didn't have my instrument rating then and there were hardly any in the plane. We would fly during the day, stopping at airfields at night, and would take taxis to our accommodation. Sometimes we saved food from breakfast to eat en route, *in an effort to cut down on costs.*

We flew on to Tunis and Tripoli and stopped at various airstrips in the desert. Flying over the remote sands for the first time was a thrilling experience but I was often diverted by looking for places to land in an emergency! Patrick managed to get permission to fly down Kitchener's railway, which was amazing, and also along the Nile, which made navigation much simpler. We could see the delta alongside the river which was lush and green, the farmers' little shacks where they all lived, and the dhows making their way through the water. I had a trip on one when we reached Luxor.

We went on to Alexandria and Cairo but when we neared Luxor we started to have trouble with the plane – the engine began "missing". We thought it was the plugs so we decided to land. There were plenty of engineers on hand with their planes – they were working on moving the Abu Simbel temple to make way for the reservoir of the Aswan High Dam –and I used my charms to get them to help us!

I was taking some pictures of our plane when the police arrived. They were very suspicious of my motives as no photographs of the Aswan were allowed to be taken and took me off to the police station. They ripped the film out of my camera and took it away – I thought I was going to be locked up but eventually they let me go. I was scared but more cross about the whole episode. However, I had actually taken three cameras with me so had two more. I persuaded a pilot from the Aswan project to take me for a flight over the site. I had put a camera up my jumper and managed to divert him while I snapped away taking illicit pictures. I have some amazing shots of the temple and the dam as mementoes and am really proud of them. I think they're probably quite valuable.

I had another hair-raising adventure in Luxor when one air traffic controller said we could stay at his flat. It was more of a shack with no running water and we had to sleep on the floor. It was quite primitive but he was so proud of it. I said I was desperate for a bath and the man said he would take me to stay at his friend's hotel instead. He drove me in his old car. The hotel was pretty awful and I felt so ill at ease that I took my handbag into the bathroom with me for safety. I managed to have a bath of sorts, after I had scrubbed it, and dried myself with the tatty little towel provided.

I eventually went to bed but was woken in the night by someone trying to get in through the window. I screamed loudly: "Captain Speedy, are you there?" and whoever it was fled but I was very frightened. I realised I could have been raped or had my passport stolen. There were some quite nice hotels locally but this was definitely seedy – I think the man and the hotel owner were in cahoots. Patrick had remained in the flat – he wasn't so desperate to have a bath – and he was very sorry about what had happened to me. I should have stayed close to him, I suppose, but you get to the point where you just must have a bath! It was a horrid experience in retrospect and I was never so careless of my safety again.

Patrick and I celebrated Christmas in Luxor. I had smuggled a pewter mug on to the Tri-pacer for Patrick which I had had engraved in Tunbridge Wells with his name and the plane's registration. I like to have things engraved to mark special events. Patrick gave me a scarf, which was far more sensible from a packing point of view.

After the holiday we went on to Khartoum where we saw the White and Blue Niles meet. It was a spectacular sight from above and amazing to see the different coloured water. However, it was in Khartoum that we suffered a devastating blow. Air Traffic Control said we couldn't go any further south as there was trouble in Djerba and we would be shot down. No light aircraft were to be allowed through. We were both floored and extremely disappointed but later, when I thought about it, I was just thrilled to have gone that far. I *was very keen to see Victoria Falls and sadly I still haven't been there but I certainly haven't ruled it out. However, our adventure was far from over…*

On the way back we took off from Tunis en route to Cagliari airport in Corsica with Patrick at the controls. We were flying across the sea and were about three-quarters of an hour into our journey when I noticed two grey gunboats below – then I saw a tracer bullet slice through the air ahead of us! They look just like fireworks and you can actually see them whizzing past. I said to Patrick: "I think those boats are firing on us," and he said: "Yes, I think they are."

It all happened very quickly. We were flying at about 3,000 feet, possibly more, so I said we should dive, which we did. Then we decided to climb, because you want to be as high as you can in those circumstances, so we did a steep climb on full throttle. This wasn't that long after I had had to study for my British licence and Neville Browning had insisted I did some aerobatic flying and also taught me how to do a short landing in a small field – all the manoeuvres I had learnt in the Auster and the Zlin certainly came in handy that day. I suggested to Patrick that we did some "leafs", dipping one wing and then the other, and reducing height and climbing again. It would have been very difficult for a gunship to home in on an aircraft carrying out those moves, particularly as our speed was much greater and its range wasn't that far.

Eventually we realised we were safe but climbed up even higher. We were pretty shaken but Patrick didn't even swear; he was a real gentleman. It was probably me who said "bloody hell" or something. Patrick was obviously perturbed but he was a very low-key type anyway, probably due to his military training!

At the time it was terrifying but it didn't last that long. When something like that happens you haven't got time to think: "Oh gosh, that could have been us in the drink." You just do what you can and then you're on your way; we didn't even go off-course. I think we upped the revs from 2.2 to 2.4 for a while, but not too long as it doesn't do the engine a lot of good. We reported it to ATC at Calgiari but they just asked a few questions and didn't seem too bothered. I never found out why the gunship crews went after us, even though Patrick phoned the MOD to report it. We assumed they were patrolling the coast because of arms movement.

It was extremely fortunate the bullets didn't hit the Tri-pacer. The wings were made essentially of "doped" fabric. I expect we could have carried on and landed if one had been damaged, but if an aileron or rudder had been hit we would have been in real trouble. I had a stiff drink at the airport while Patrick went off to Air Traffic Control to do all the paperwork.

Although I was sad the trip was cut short, I was quite glad to go home and, after the gunboat incident, to be in one piece. I had felt homesick a lot of the time. It was an absolutely exhilarating experience but I kept thinking how much the family would have enjoyed it all and tried to send a postcard from every stopover. I took home a traditional decorated leather pouffe which I still have. They are flat so are easy to transport – you stuff them yourself with newspapers. I also bought some miniature straw camels. We couldn't take back anything heavy but I gave Jamie an Arab suit complete with "tea-cloth" headdress for dressing-up parties and I took Elizabeth a leather hat. The children were delighted with their presents and I showed them the route Patrick and I had taken on maps. They were both enthralled by flying even then and it was only a short while afterwards that I began to teach Jamie to fly.

The trip took 97 flying hours altogether. Patrick and I got on relatively well, bearing in mind that we were cooped up in an aeroplane for all that time. He always wanted to do the landings but after a while I said: "Now come on, this is my turn." He also criticised my navigation at one point and said we were off by five miles. I argued with him about that – I was bang on track! However, my ego received an amusing and welcome boost when we landed in Egypt. The ground staff insisted on calling me "Captain – Captain Diana Freeman". I looked around to see who they meant – I wasn't used to that! I told them I wasn't a captain but it made no difference. They said: "But you fly a plane. You are a captain!"

We had stopped at Tunis on the way out and my attention had been caught by a stationary fleet of Dragon Rapides, the twin-engined biplanes that are still used on routes to the Channel Islands. In those days they were quite rare and I thought if one could have been crated up and taken to Headcorn and rebuilt it would have been a good investment.

One had been brought to the farm by a commercial pilot and I went up in it with him and flew it for a while. The Dragon Rapide looks a bit like a Tiger Moth. It's a single cockpit and the pilot "trimmed" it out and I flew it straight and level – it was a lovely plane to fly. It had a lavatory in the back and the pilot confessed he used to trim it out and go to the loo and come back again, not something that anyone was likely to approve of! It's very important to trim a plane out properly, in case one felt ill while flying for example, and I did it automatically. I wanted to buy that plane but Chris, probably wisely, had reservations and advised me not to do so.

Rye Bay Riot

I had always loved sailing – in 1966 I was pictured in my bikini on a Shamrock catamaran on the front cover of The Helmsman. *Two years earlier I crewed for John Thompson when he won the Golden Miller cup in the Round the Island race at the Isle of Wight. Chris had entered the Fastnet race before I met him and so I decided to buy an ex-naval, clinker-built pinnace called Sunstream from George Roberts, who was head of the River Board in Rye. He had converted the boat into a cutter, or fast sailing boat. We kept it on a swing mooring at Rye and added otter boards so that we could trawl for fish.*

I taught the children to sail and loved taking them out in Rye Bay, but I was absolutely terrified in case they fell overboard so I always tied them to the mast or the stern while we were tacking or going about!

We loved to sail Sunstream across to Boulogne, sometimes taking the children with us. Bassin Loubet, where we used to moor, was tidal and you had to climb a ladder up to the quayside. We would go off to buy some duty-frees, which had to be lowered down to the boat on a rope. These were called "bonded stores" then and we were supposed to have a special place to lock them away on board, but we never did.

On one occasion Chris and I went over to Boulogne in our boat and another of my adopted "uncles", Uncle Dick, came in his beautiful fibreglass sailing boat, after I had persuaded a friend, David Carr Taylor, from the Sussex wine-making family, to crew for him. We tied up and got our duty-free allowance but on the way back there was a bit of a storm, to put it mildly. It blew out two sails and we were left with just the foresail, which did at least manage to keep the boat steady. There were breeches buoys – rope-based rescue devices for people on stricken vessels – out all along the coast because of the conditions and Chris and I put our life jackets on, which we rarely did. The water pump couldn't cope and we were shipping water which I was madly trying to bail out while Chris was struggling to keep the engine going and keep muck out of the fuel. Apparently Uncle Dick left David to do most of the work on their boat while he went below and started swigging brandy!

I thought we would have to beach at Camber but we eventually managed to limp up Rye Channel. When we reached the harbour master's at Rye we were supposed to fly a yellow flag to alert the customs. I only had a yellow duster so I put that up and the customs officers came to check what we had on board.

But Uncle Dick went to the other side of the channel! His boat had no deep keel and he told David to take the boat up the slipway there. David said: "I can't. We've got to clear customs." But Uncle Dick said: "Do as I say!" so David did. The customs officers were furious and had to go over to the other side of the channel to remonstrate with him. When they told him they wanted to see what he had brought back, Uncle Dick said: "You can't. I've drunk it all." And he had, more or less!

After that nerve-racking escapade we fell into the pub and drank too much ourselves, I'm sorry to say, before driving home, as we did in those days.

The Bentley

During a rare family holiday to the West Country I bought a Bentley on a whim! I had always lusted after one, ever since I had worked on Bill Mason's beautiful sports version in my racing days. I spotted a Parkward 2.5 litre sports saloon in Brixham. I was admiring it when the old gentleman to whom it belonged came out and said it was for sale. I think it cost about £700; today it would be worth a fortune. It had a "straight-through" exhaust; you pulled a lever and it went straight through; it sounded amazing! Chris thought it would be fun to have it but pointed out that the tyres weren't in very good condition. We checked it over thoroughly before we bought it and everything else was fine.

We had gone on holiday in our Austin shooting brake and had to drive home in convoy. On the way we found two women from Pluckley in Kent who had broken down and we picked them up. The Bentley was completely loaded up with their stuff and ours; the cot was on the roof. I was worried the whole way home about the tyres bursting but we managed the journey safely, thank heavens. The first thing I did when we reached home was to change the tyres! Sadly I had to sell the Bentley when I was short of money.

Neville's Browning's Christmas card, showing him upside down in the Slin

Neville's Slin was his 'skin'

Army Air Corps helicopters practising their waltz at Headcorn in preparation for air displays that they put on all over Britain and Europe

Me pictured flying along the beach at Le Touquet. I don't think it was allowed!

We loved our hopfields and the characters who came to work on them every summer
Kent Messenger

The dinner following the Deauville rally. I was cross as the female helicopter pilots got more attention than me

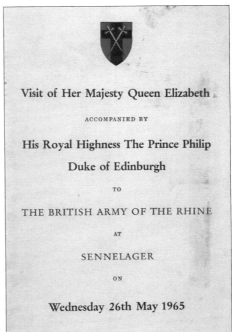

We flew to this glamorous event in the Auster and stayed on base with Major Mike Somerton-Rayner, CO of the Army Air Corps

Left: Cover girl on
The Helmsman,
January 1966

Below: At work on the
new Auster, the latest
addition to our 'fleet'.
Daily Sketch

Pashley, who owned the flying club at Shoreham Airport, was a dear friend and great character. Pictured second from right with friends, the year before he died

Pashley let me fly ACDC, the oldest Tiger Moth in existence, when it was kept at Shoreham

*Being greeted by the family,
Hoppy the dog included,
after a I flew in from a
shopping trip. It really was
cheaper to go by plane.*
Daily Mirror

*Chris - tie carefully tucked in – helps
me get going. The door was off to
enable me to take photographs*
Daily Mirror

*Me pictured from above,
flying over our house at
Headcorn at under 100 feet.*
Daily Mirror

Modelling for a Canterbury store

Flying in to Shoreham to publicise the ice rink in Brighton.
The Argus, Brighton.

Elegant on the ice – I did a lot of skating at my finishing school in Switzerland, Chatelard
The Argus, Brighton.

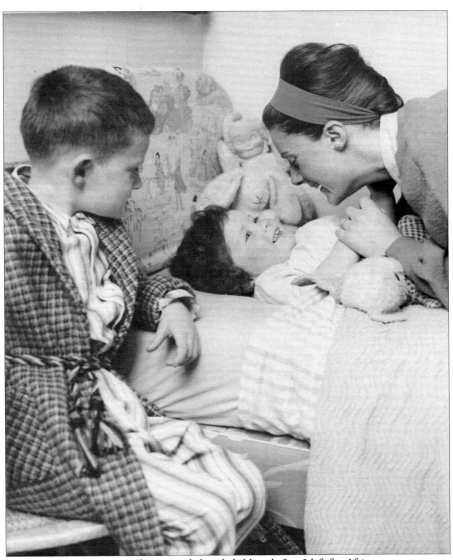

Saying goodbye to my beloved children before I left for Africa.
Daily Mirror

Planning our route to Africa. Chris was happy for me to go on an adventure with Patrick Speedy while he minded the farm.
Daily Mirror

Setting off with Patrick in the Tri-pacer for our African trip.
***Daily Express**.*

My picture of one of Sardinia's megalithic nuraghes taken from the Tri-pacer

A refuelling stop in the desert

The Marble Arch

Moving part of the Abu Simbel temple by barge

*I was really proud of these pictures I took in Africa of the
Aswan High Dam project and the Abu Simbel temples.
The authorities confiscated one of my cameras, but fortunately I had two more!*

The great Sphinx at Giza

I got the opportunity to go sightseeing on our African trip and went riding in the desert and took a trip on a dhow on the Nile

I missed my animals on the farm but befriending a camel made up for it

Home again. Showing Elizabeth where Mummy had been in Africa
Kent News and Photo Agency.

My lovely boat Sunstream, in which we all had such fun,
hopping across the Channel and sailing in Rye Bay

The Bentley – and Hoppy

Headcorn: Down to Earth with a Bump

Chris and I had so much going for us. Life was exciting: we had a lovely home, planes, cars, a thriving farm, a successful airfield that was gaining in reputation and two wonderful children. But, from my point of view, it was my much-loved husband's limitations as a father that finally drove us apart.

As the years went on he seemed to stop taking any real interest in the children and it was always left to me to organise and make decisions about their education, which I found extremely frustrating and hurtful. He was always "too busy" even to look round possible schools for them, and this kept on happening. Matters grew worse between us. He began staying in the pub late and, if we had a dinner party, he would turn up in his farming overalls and embarrass me. We used to do a lot of entertaining and often had 16 for dinner, but he started treating it all as a joke, even though, when he was "on song", he was an excellent host and enjoyed it all. Eventually I met someone else who adored the children and that, I suppose, was the beginning of the end. We separated in 1969.

A typical example of how Chris continued to disappoint us was when he promised to take the Duck, an amphibious vehicle from the farm, to Jamie's prep school, St Andrew's in Eastbourne, on his last day there – but it didn't happen. I had sold my XK140, because I needed some money, a decision that I later regretted. When Chris let Jamie down over the Duck I rushed out and, rather impetuously I suppose, bought a Jensen Healey, which had a Lotus engine, so that our son would have something to be proud of in front of his school friends. (I later took the Jensen up to Lotus on the old RAF Hethel base in Norfolk where the company had its workshops and did some trials for them on the airfield there.)

Chris didn't come to Jamie's last day, even though Margaret Thatcher was the guest of honour and Jamie, who led the choir, was to sing a solo. Mrs Thatcher was then the Minister for Education and had come to open the new school hall. Jamie sang *The Lord's Prayer*. Mrs Thatcher loved it: she told him he sang beautifully and asked if he could sing something else. The music teacher leapt into action and Jamie did sing another piece, but the schedule had obviously been timed to the last minute and the whole thing was thrown out! Mrs Thatcher then presented Jamie with the Music Cup. I was so thrilled and proud, and so sad that Chris hadn't seen his son's bravura performance. Jamie wasn't allowed to keep the cup so I had a replica made.

We all had lunch and Mrs Thatcher made a speech in which she praised the former head and his wife, Philip and Jane Liddell. Mr Liddell was headmaster from 1946-1969 and Mrs Thatcher referred to Mrs Liddell's exceptional ability to source items that had become unavailable because of the war. Iron bedsteads had been commandeered as part of the war effort, but Mrs Liddell had still managed to find some, saving the boys from having to sleep on the floor.

As was the tradition when a child left, we made a presentation to the school; we chose a piano. We donated a payphone to Elizabeth's school, Beresford House, in Eastbourne.

When I moved out of the farm I took precious little from it, even though I had invested a lot of my own money in improving our living accommodation and building up the airfield. But, fortunately, I had a bolt hole, my little coastguard cottage by the sea, where I could have the children when they were home from school. I had got to know Pett Level, near Winchelsea, in East Sussex, as a child. My Uncle Dick, a vet, used to stay at The Cove pub in nearby Fairlight with my aunt Dorothy. It was a very upmarket establishment then with beautiful rooms and wonderful food. Sometimes I would go and stay there, too.

We got to know a lot of people locally and I loved it there – it was an idyllic place for a child. There were very few houses but on the seafront at Pett Level there was a row of tiny coastguard cottages. I used to gaze at them and say: "If I ever have a cottage I'd like one like that." Years later, one of them, Number 5, was to become my permanent home.

In the early Sixties, when I was at Headcorn, the telephone had rung and a Mrs Young, who owned two of the coastguard cottages and whom I had got to know, was on the other end. She was very brisk and came straight to the point: "Diana," she said. "I'm selling Number 5. Do you want it?" We didn't tend to have summer breaks and I had thought it would be nice to have somewhere to take the children in their school holidays, but the phone call came at 8 o'clock at night and it was such a surprise that I ummed and aahed and dithered a bit. But Mrs Young barked brusquely: "If you don't, there are several who do. I need to know *now*." So I found myself saying yes!

I contacted my bank manager the next morning, who said: "Oh dear, Diana!", but then seemed to think it was quite a sensible investment. Number 5 was already well over 100 years old at that stage and I paid several thousand for it. It was furnished and I had to have the furniture with it, quite a bit of which I discarded. The cottage had a ladder up to the top floor which I replaced with a substantial staircase made by the local builder, Mr Scotcher. There was an old bath upstairs with an ancient gas geyser that provided hot water. The flue went through the outside wall and over Granny Crumpton's one-storey cottage next door. You had to light the pilot light to get hot water – the flame would flare up and there would be an alarming "whoomfh" sound. I was convinced it was dangerous and wouldn't have the children at the cottage until it had been replaced.

I bought a lovely, large new bath and had that installed. I dismantled and removed an old fireplace with green shiny tiles, which didn't fit in with my furniture, but it turned out that Mrs Young had been very fond of it so, when her daughter saw it standing in the garden she asked if she could have it, and so it went back to someone who loved it.

Two years after I bought Number 5 the drive at the end of the cottages came up for sale. My friend, Betty Gostic, told me about it and I bought that. I was very pleased as I needed a garage to house my old 2.5 Park Ward sports saloon and the River Board, which owned the track (now a road) that ran past the cottages, gave me permission to build one. Some while later a tiny little cottage, Marigold, came up for sale three doors away. I bought that, too, much to the detriment of my poor bank manager's nerves, but it, too, turned out to be a good investment. I painted the door tangerine, as I did my sitting-room ceiling, to remind me of my Dauphin; it has become one of my favourite colours. I have since made Marigold over to Jamie and Number 5 to Elizabeth.

Before I bought the cottages I had put in a bid for Stonewalls, the quirky "castle" overlooking the sea at Cliff End. Uncle Paddy, an architect, looked it over for me but I was outbid by Peter Woodroffe who became a friend. He had inherited Green Shutters, which was later sold to Gordon and Jean Farrer, who were also my friends. Jean was brilliant at interior design and made a wonderful job of the house.

I loved being at Pett Level – when I took over the cottage the area was very different and felt quite remote. There were few dwellings, they were mostly picturesque little shacks like Marigold. Sometimes the River Board closed the track from Winchelsea Beach for maintenance on the sea wall or something similar, and then one had to access the village via Winchelsea and Chick Hill, quite a roundabout route. The children thought that was great fun.

We spent many happy times at the cottage. My Uncle Dick knew the Jacksons, who owned the Two Sawyers pub, well and they remained my friends. The children became close to their children. The Jacksons had one of the first televisions in the village so Jamie would often disappear with their son Simon to watch it.

The Farrers lived briefly at No 3 Coastguard Cottages and Gordon, a jeweller, was a very good piano player. We had some marvellous sing-songs: I would play my ukulele, which I still have. One of my tennis partners, John Farmer, played the guitar. He lived at Old Surrenden Manor in Bethersden and I persuaded him to have a floodlit tennis court put in. I was fond of his mother, Dorothy, and did my best to help her before she died of cancer.

We all went sailing in the bay and water-skiing at the lakes out towards Camber. We had some great parties at the Coastguard Cottages, too. I had hundreds of records.

We were all so pally along here in those days. We would just walk into each other's houses if we needed something, take it and leave a note! Dilys, who lived next door, and I would baby-sit for each other – we had an intercom set up between our cottages.

Pett Level is a beautiful area but has often been under threat from over-development as, sadly, it still is today. At one stage there was a plan to have a caravan park, funfair and ice-cream parlour just opposite the Coastguard Cottages, but the local people got together to form a preservation society, the Pett Level Trust, and managed to ward off the threat by buying the land. The Goldsmiths, who owned the village shop, were involved, as were Cecily Perring and Angela Hawkesley; Kitty Leaver from the little cottage Tamarisk across the way was the secretary. We all did a lot of fund-raising and used to organise fetes and similar events to boost the communal bank balance, with Betty and Ron Wakeham. Ron was the treasurer and later Robin took over. I still have my residence receipt for 2s 6d.

There were many characters in Pett Level. Fay Godwin, the landscape photographer, was an amazing woman who could talk on any subject. Marion Ling, who lived at Toot Rock and worked hard for the Pett Level Trust, was impeccably dressed until the day she died, in her nineties. She had been in advertising and was so courteous and amusing. She always offered guests coffee or tea but they usually ended up having a sherry with her!

I do pray that this very special place isn't eventually ruined by greed and unsuitable over-expansion.

A portrait of me by Spencer Roberts, a well-known painter who lived at Fairlight
and worked locally as an art teacher.
His largest work was a mural for the Manor House at Port Lympne

Robin was tall, handsome and, to the delight of Jamie and Elizabeth
he liked speed as much as they did!

Heartbreak, Romance... and Robin

After Chris and I separated I had another relationship, which had been happy but ended sadly, so, while the children were away at school, I used to spend quite a bit of time at the Two Sawyers and knew a lot of people in there. One evening I was talking to some friends and they said: "Have you met Jack?" They introduced me to Jack Watsham, who had a farm at Westfield, and we hit it off straight away. We were both into farming and Jack was tall and good-looking. The evening ended with me asking him if he would like to come for coffee at the cottage and he said that would be nice!

We got on very well and eventually Jack invited me to go to see his home, Pattletons Farm, and meet Robert, his son. I remember driving down a long lane and seeing this lovely old house. The farm was very well managed and Jack kept pigs which, of course, I knew a lot about, having had them at Headcorn. The woods were filled with bluebells in the spring and it was all quite idyllic.

Jack and I became very fond of each other. I got on very well with Robert; he treated me like a second mother and used to love to tease me. The children all liked each other and Jack gave Jamie a small piece of the farm, which he spent hours clearing. Jack even had a document beautifully drawn up and Jamie was very proud of it.

They were very happy days – Jack nicknamed me Scruff because of the farming gear I used to wear. He loved my cooking, as did Robert and his girlfriend, Angela Hickman, and we had many fun meals together. Jack said he wanted to marry me and he asked Chris if he approved – he said yes. Jack even persuaded me to change my name to Watsham legally. Jack's parents had a lovely house on the farm. We became very fond of each other and I helped them quite a bit – I remember Jack's mother telling the farm staff and friends: "There's another Mrs Watsham on the farm!"

I made some changes to the house, putting in another bathroom and two bedrooms in the attic so that Jamie and Elizabeth could stay and have some space. I bought a huge bath for the main bathroom, which Jack and I used to bathe in together, and managed to get the old one up into the attic bathroom with the help of Mr Previtt, who lived in Ore. He was an old-fashioned builder/carpenter of the "you name it, he could do it" ilk. David and Peter were two brothers who worked on the farm and were very good to me and there was a lovely lady who worked in the old farm house and really cared for the place.

Jack and I had a memorable holiday in a wonderful hotel by the sea in southern Cyprus. We hired a car and went to visit a remote monastery. As we bumped up this unmade track Jack said: "Just as well this isn't your car, Scruff. You would never have driven it up here!" He knew I was very protective about my precious car – I had a Fiat 124 Sport at the time. The monks were very pleased to see us and, assuming we were married, they blessed us and gave us some of their own homemade wine – it was a good job Jack was driving on the way back!

In the evenings we changed for dinner. Jack would go to the bar first and I would make myself as glamorous as possible and he was so proud when I entered the room. The meals were excellent and we would dance afterwards; Jack was a very good dancer and very proud of me when the band asked me to do their national dance with them.

We went up to the Troodos Mountains and skied, stayed in a log cabin and joined in all the fun on the slopes. We both agreed it had been a wonderful holiday.

I helped Robert to get his first job, in an international bank in the City – he was very good at languages. We went up to London with him for the interview and were all very smartly dressed, Robert tall and handsome in his new suit and me suitably attired for the occasion in suit, hat and gloves. Afterwards we had lunch and walked to Trafalgar Square, where we took a picture of Robert with the pigeons; I was desperately hoping they wouldn't poo on his lovely suit!

When he was 21 I organised his party at the flat that he shared in Putney and persuaded Jack to buy him a green Mini. I transported all the food, flowers and cake to London with Angela in Jack's lovely, roomy car. I made him take his parents in the little Mini because his mother smoked and Angela and I said the food would be contaminated – she and I did laugh about it!

I was very happy, but it was not to last. When Jack had to go away on business for part of his work he would phone every evening to talk to me and see how things were on the farm. However, I should have guessed that something was wrong when he said: "Must go, Scruff; there's a line-up for the phone." Even in those days there were phones in hotel rooms... He was, of course, seeing someone else.

When it all came out I was terribly unhappy; we had been together for three years and it was a dreadful shock. I cried and cried and all our friends were very upset, too, although one had warned me that Jack wasn't right for me. Jack and his new girlfriend stayed together and married; he converted one of the barns into a beautiful new house for them and sold some of the land. However, when he was dying, he asked to see me. He held my hand and said: "Sorry, Scruff." I got into my car and wept all the way back to the cottage at Pett Level. Then I had a large drink.

Jack died in 1995 and was buried in the bluebell wood which he loved and where we used to walk every day. Robert, who has two wonderful children, a daughter, Louise, and a son, Patrick, had his grandparents' home eventually but it was sold when he was divorced, which was a great shame. I always felt sad that he didn't inherit the bluebell wood or the farm where Jack was buried. Jack and I always said that one day the farm would be his and I had promised to help him with it. Jack's wife inherited his property and Robert was unable even to buy the piece of land where his father was buried. The property was eventually sold. I could not believe how it worked out and was extremely upset about it, particularly for Robert.

The one good thing to come out of all the sadness surrounding the affair is that Robert and I have remained close and he is also still friendly with Jamie, with whom he shares sporting interests.

After Jack, I was living alone at Pett Level and just getting on with my life as best I could with the children when, in 1973, the three of us were invited to a New Year's Eve party at High Halden in Kent by our friends, the Austins. I helped out with the catering and thought I might go to bed early after everyone had eaten, but Doreen Austin said: "Don't be ridiculous, Di. Come and join the party." So, somewhat resignedly, I did as I was bid.

What I didn't realise was that there was another reluctant guest – Robin. He had been staying with his brother, Peter, and his wife, Sue, at their home, The Paddocks, in nearby Hothfield, and had also been jollied into attending the party. Robin asked me to dance. He was wearing a dinner jacket borrowed from his brother and, as he is 6ft 3in, the sleeves ended half-way up his arms! I managed to persuade our hosts to allow the men to discard their jackets, much to Robin's relief. I remember I got hiccups. Robin said the best way to cure them was with a kiss… We were married the following year.

A Seventies-style picture of Robin and me

Country Life

When I met Robin I was in fact seeing another man, an airline pilot named Derek Butcher, who worked for Gulf Air. We got on extremely well as we had flying in common and we would talk about it for hours. He wanted to marry me and had a wedding ring made; he also gave me a beautiful caftan embroidered in gold but, unfortunately, he was based in Dubai, which did rather complicate things.

At that time I was driving an old Fiat that Chris had given me to cart the children's school trunks around in and which I did up. Both Robin and Derek used to take the wheel when we went out. Derek used to drive it quite carefully and slowly, while Robin, who drove a fast Ford of his own, was much racier. The children were used to speed and when Derek was driving they would be sitting in the back making shoving motions with their hands, trying to move the car forward more quickly. When I told them that Derek wanted to marry me they said: "No! You must marry Robin because he can *drive*!"

Robin got on very well with my children and was a great help and support, which I felt Chris hadn't been in later years. He actually had four sons of his own from a former marriage and they often came to visit, which was great fun.

We decided to marry quite quickly, although my dear aunt Mim cautioned me against it. "He's a *golfer*," she said darkly. "A golfer is always a golfer. You'll be a golf widow!" The ceremony was at Battle register office and the reception at my cottage in Pett Level. We managed to squeeze 70 people in, once we had taken the bed out of what is now the dining room! Aunt Mim paid for the wedding breakfast, which I helped my good friend, Ba Kielly, to prepare. Everyone said what a lovely party it was, and the cottage did provide an idyllic setting with the sea and cliffs as a backdrop. Aunt Mim also paid for us to spend a night at the Grand Hotel in Eastbourne, which was wonderful.

Robin, who had been to Winchester like his father, Mark, was an agricultural merchant and had a Victorian house, Libra, in an acre of land near East Dereham, in Norfolk, so we made our home there. His former mother-in-law lived with him; she didn't take too kindly to me, but when she became ill I nursed her and, I think, changed her opinion of me. When she eventually had to move into a nursing home I was the only one she wanted to see.

Jamie and Elizabeth had their own bedrooms at Libra, as did three of Robin's sons, Matthew, Simon and William. His youngest child, Luke, was considered too young to stay. The boys were all at Woolverstone Hall School in Suffolk and I often used to go there to watch the boys' matches and to take tea down. William had a Mirror dinghy and I used to help him transport it. Jamie and Elizabeth were still at their boarding schools in Sussex, but would come up in the holidays and we would often decamp to Pett Level at weekends. Robin became a member of Rye Golf Club, as his father had been, so that was a great attraction, too. It was incredible the number of miles we did back and forth. We always left Number 5 immaculate so that it would be welcoming on our return.

I was more or less a housewife and nurse in those days and was also busy looking after all the children. I attempted to play golf but I was never great at it – my handicap was 36 – but I enjoyed it because I was with Robin. We belonged to East Dereham while we were in Norfolk and later, when we moved to Suffolk, to Stoke by Nayland. On one memorable occasion, during a business trip to America with Robin, I actually managed a hole in one!

I used to take Matthew to play at a course on Fakenham racecourse. We would go round and round the nine holes, often until it got dark. I used to say: "I must go home and get Daddy's supper," and Matthew would say: "Oh no, just a few more holes, Di!"

Despite being involved in so many other things I hadn't forgotten about my flying. I kept my licence going and when I moved to Norfolk I used to fly at Swanton Morley flying club and would always hire the same Cessna 172, so I could get to know it better. Having had my own plane I was extremely fussy. I took Robin's children up as a treat during the holidays, although the responsibility terrified me – the *whole family*, imagine! – but I always did a circuit first and carried out my own inspections. My friends at the flying club used to tease "old fusspot Annie" about it but I certainly wasn't prepared to take any risks with such a precious cargo. However, Robin had total confidence in me and I used to fly him around frequently so that he could inspect the crops from the air. He was involved in weed control and needed to see how the wheat was faring, for instance, and report back to the farmers who were his customers. Seeing it all from an aeroplane gave a completely different perspective which Robin found extremely useful – he became well known for doing it and so did I.

On one occasion I was approached to take up a photographer who was helping to compile a book called *Nature in Norfolk, A Heritage in Trust*, which was published by Jarrold and contained pieces from various contributors and a foreword by Sir Peter Scott. I think the flying club exaggerated my capabilities but the company was told I was the right person for the job. Aerial photography was virtually unheard of in those days and I used the opportunity to take some fascinating pictures of my own.

Robin was eventually made MD of his company, Stimpson Pertwee, but then, in 1976, he was promoted to MD of the Pertwee Group in Colchester, which meant that we needed to move house. As he was busily involved in his new job, I set off to find a new home in the Jensen, getting up at 6am – sometimes I slept in the car to save money. The search took me three months: I was looking within a 30 mile radius of Colchester. I used to go into village pubs to talk to the locals in my favoured area, which proved to be an excellent idea. They warned me off one house I liked because it was too close to a piggery and could be smelly if the wind was in the wrong direction. Robin came to see another, a lovely farm that I really liked, but we viewed it at night, fortunately, and found that it was lit up by the glare from all the sodium lighting in Colchester.

Eventually the locals in a pub in Kersey, in Suffolk, pointed me towards Primrose Cottage in Groton and I fell in love with it. It had a curved drive – Mummy used to say, "always have a curved drive so that the house is a lovely surprise". Robin liked it, too, and we became involved in a race to buy it as others were interested. I did all the searches myself except for a couple of points with which I was helped by a solicitor's clerk and, in the end, we got there first and bought it. It was 16th century, pale green, with barley-sugar chimneys, had four bedrooms and two bathrooms and was set in about 15 acres. All the children had their own space and we kept the spare room beautifully prepared for Robin's parents to come to stay.

There were two small lakes and I installed a water feature as a present for Robin but my "romantic gesture" kept going wrong and I frequently had to go into the water in my swimming costume and waders to try to sort it out. We also had ducks and a thatched duck house, which was weighted to ensure it stayed put in the middle of the lake.

The cottage had a tennis court and as I was quite an accomplished player – I always got my ball – the boys and I made good use of it. I used to play doubles with Robin and we took part in a local tournament among all the people who had their own courts. In one we were doing brilliantly; we were in the finals and the other couple, who were county standard and played much more than we did, seemed a little put out. There was a bit of an atmosphere and one of our opponents slammed a ball that hit me in the chest. It certainly hurt and winded me a bit, but nothing was broken so I just got on with it although Robin was furious and slammed a killer ball back. They beat us after a ferocious battle and in the presentation all we received were three tennis balls for our efforts – Robin was convinced they were last year's as well!

I was idyllically happy in Groton and reverted to farming, albeit on a smaller scale. I really missed my sheep when I left Headcorn and for our seventh "woollen" wedding anniversary Robin gave me three huge Border Leicester's, which he named after me:

Diana, Mary and Ava. I used to breed from them and ended up with a flock of 90 sheep, including pure Suffolks, which I sold on for breeding and producing. I took care of them all myself and also looked after other people's sheep, too, including checking their feet, mouths and the lambing.

Robin was more used to crops but he began to get into animal farming, too. I lost only two of my own lambs: one fell in a water butt and the other was sickly with a cleft mouth. It needed to be put to sleep and when I rang the vet he said briskly: "You can do it yourself; I'll give you the injection." I didn't want to and asked Robin if he would hold the lamb for me while I injected it but he said: "I'm sorry, I can't", so I did it on my own but I hated every second and was terribly sad. I buried the poor lamb in the garden.

We also built a sheep dip and dipped everyone's sheep for miles around. When we finally left Primrose Cottage our Suffolk purebreds went down to Headcorn and were absorbed into Jamie's flock.

I rode when I could – there was a local point-to-point stables and I was one of several people who used to exercise the horses there. My favourite was named Typena and I have a picture of her – she was beautiful. Eventually Robin built a pole barn and some stables, which I designed and, at long last, I got my own horse, Rosie. She was 16.2 hands out of a Clydesdale mare by the premium stallion Thatch and she was given to me by a friend, Jay Swallow, who was an author and had written about Rosie's sister, Cider Rose.

She said Rosie wouldn't be much use as she had a cleft hoof and I'd never get her right but I saw that as a challenge. I worked on her with the aid of the local blacksmith, Roger Clarke, and put her on a special diet. I gave her an excellent supplement called Drive which Elizabeth, who, by that time was living in America, sent me. Although Rosie's affected foot was half an inch smaller across than the other three I managed to get her totally sound and she was perfect to ride – I used to hunt and show her; she could jump anything. We tended to stick to one-day events but I won countless rosettes with her.

Rosie was very special and turned into the most amazing ride and wonderful, loving companion. Everyone adored her but she and I had a special bond and she actually saved my life on two occasions. She was such a part of the family that she would wander in through the front door of Primrose Cottage and out through the back, stopping only for a snack in the kitchen on the way.

I used to take her to Towerlands Equestrian Centre in Essex and she was the first horse to go round its cross-country course. She was terribly spoilt and while we were there we would rent a stable for her so that she had her own little pad, rather than tie her to her trailer!

I studied dressage for a week with the expert Lady Sylvia Loch at an amazing baronial hall in East Anglia. There were grooms to look after the horses but Rosie was such a mummy's girl that I used to get up at dawn to go and look after her myself. Rosie adapted brilliantly to the discipline and in fact, on one occasion, her skill saved my life – for the first time. After we had all moved back to Sussex I was riding her out when a lorry came careering towards us. I thought we had had it but I managed to think quickly enough to give Rosie the appropriate aids and she side-stepped up a steep bank, carrying us both out of the path of the oncoming vehicle. Sylvia mentioned the incident in one of her brilliant books on dressage and said she was very proud of her novice pupil and her clever horse. I was so keen on the discipline that Robin built me a dressage arena at Primrose Cottage and when we moved to Pett Level he would set up stones for me on the beach so that I could continue practising.

While we were in Suffolk we did a lot of entertaining. I had a lovely Aga – it was my pride and joy and I had it raised up on plinths so it was the perfect height for me to use. I became involved with the local Conservatives and prepared food for branch events. I became social secretary and helped raise a lot of money. Both our local MPs were quite controversial figures: Selwyn Gummer, now Lord Deben, who was later criticised for feeding his young daughter a hamburger to try to allay fears during the BSE scandal, was the MP for the Suffolk Coastal region, and Tim Yeo, whose two love children caused tongues to wag, was MP for South Suffolk. If you got Tim away from politics, he was great fun. He was good-looking and a bit of a ladies' man but we didn't discuss his private life. We used to have extremely formal party meetings at the home of the party chairman, Richard Meyers – we weren't even allowed water, let alone a chance to gossip! Robin wasn't interested in politics at all until then so it was my fault he got into it eventually.

Sadly, though, our Suffolk idyll was destined not to last. In 1986 Robin was unfortunately made redundant. We tried very hard to stay at Primrose Cottage – I worked slavishly with the sheep, which kept Rosie and the family going for a bit, and Robin became a sort of upmarket salesman for X-ergon, an American utilities company. I became his secretary and would sit up in bed, surrounded by paperwork and maps, trying to impress his potential clients with my pleasant voice and efficient telephone manner. When making appointments I would say: "I'll see if that will suit Mr Patten's diary," in a very imposing way! Robin would arrive looking extremely smart in a business suit, carrying a case full of samples. He worked very hard but, in the end, we couldn't keep the house and we were forced to face the future. As it had done before, No 5 Coastguards provided a safe and welcoming haven – and so we packed up all our belongings and moved back down to the sea.

Primrose Cottage in Suffolk where Robin and I made our home.
It was such a beautiful house and I loved it there

Aunt Mim and Nicky, Uncle Peter's son, tackle the paddock at Primrose Cottage

Elizabeth and Jamie with the Prichards at Sand Lake when Robin and I took the children to Canada to meet them

On the golf course where I had my only hole in one!
I achieved this great feat in America; Robin and I were there on a business trip

My Jensen Healey

Robin's parents, Mark and Peggy, with me and Walter, our Yorkshire Terrier

Sea Change

Returning to live in my little cottage by the sea had its pros and cons. Although its position is enviable, it *is* compact and we had an awful lot of treasures, such as fine paintings of our relatives and ancestors; myriad mementoes from childhood and of my flying; artefacts and furniture from The Firs, including the vast dining table that seated 16, which I had used at Headcorn, and a beautiful but huge antique chest belonging to Robin. Somehow we managed to fit most of it into No 5.

Over the years we have altered and changed the layout. In the early days we rented the cottage next door while we had the old conservatory knocked down and a sitting room built in its place. Fortunately, we also have Marigold close by, which we use as Robin's office and as guest accommodation, so we have been able to utilise some of our furniture and other possessions in there.

I converted the garage next to Marigold into a stable for Rosie, with the help of Mr Previtt. Rosie used the garden of Marigold as a play area. She also had a shelter in a nearby field but I would bring her to Marigold for the night if I was planning to ride her the next day or take her off somewhere in the trailer. (I later converted her stable at Marigold into a gym for me, aided by local builder Jimmy Harris.)

Once back in Sussex, Robin and I needed to make a living and we decided to buy a small company, Jamie Wood Ltd, in Polegate, near Eastbourne. We bought it from a man named Jamie McTear, who built the original bird hide at Rye Nature Reserve – we kept a model of it in the showroom.

The company specialised in making hides, bird boxes and bird tables and I thoroughly enjoyed it. Robin has always been very skilled in woodwork and I also did a lot of the construction – I did everything apart from the sawing and part of the bird box roofs, which were complicated.

We had a great staff – I was particularly fond of Mary, who did the packing, and we became friends. We refitted a caravan that we owned and we would tow it with my old Volvo, travelling round to craft shows and country fairs with our goods, and living in it while we were there. We went to the big bird fair at Rutland Water for five years running and it was tremendous fun.

Robin and I had the company for several years, but then the daily drive to Polegate became too much and, rather sadly, we decided to give it up. But we had made lots of lovely pieces of which we were proud and we still have several of the bird boxes dotted around our garden.

And so we settled down to a different kind of life. Robin's parents, Mark and Peggy, lived at Hove which meant we were closer to them but eventually they moved a few doors away from us, to a house that was named Pebbles. It was replaced by The White House, which was built by Tom Watkins, the former manager of the pop group the Pet Shop Boys, and was featured on Channel 4's *Grand Designs* programme. We put a wet room and ramps into Pebbles. I used to cook for my parents-in-law and when they became ill I helped nurse them both for six years.

Peggy went into hospital for a relatively minor stomach operation, which was successful, but she got an infection in her leg that turned septic, then gangrenous. As a result, her leg had to be amputated at the knee. She was so good about it and "Pa", Mark, helped her all the way. Peggy had a motorised wheelchair that she handled with aplomb although the doorways and furniture got a bit of a bashing, but she even managed to do some gardening from it – her great love – tending to her raised flower beds. With my medical background it wasn't too hard for me to deal with bedpans etc. In later years I was often called on to nurse other people in the village, and I still look after sick friends if needed.

Mark had set up a division of Beechams, the pharmaceutical company, in Australia and Robin was born there. Mark had been a member of Rye Golf Club and, just before we moved to Pett Level, Robin joined and he eventually became Captain. I was proposed by a friend later on and I joined, too. It's a beautiful course in a superb setting and we won one or two matches while I was with the ladies.

Robin had been drawn into politics through my involvement in Suffolk. When we moved back to Sussex I joined the Hastings and Rye Conservative Association and Robin became even more involved, leading to him becoming chairman. He was then elected a Rother District councillor in 1999, was chairman in 2007 and remains deputy leader of the council.

When Robin was chairman of the RDC it meant a full social calendar and I accompanied him to all kinds of different events. Unfortunately I already had plenty of suitable clothes so couldn't justify a new wardrobe!

Robin opened Rye swimming pool and we had dinner with Alastair Ainslie, the High Sheriff of East Sussex. As council chairman Robin received an invitation to one of the Buckingham Palace garden parties. We were in the line-up to meet Prince Philip. I remember he was extremely uncomplimentary about one gentleman's rather florid tie: "Woolworths, I presume," he said, in typically acerbic fashion.

I had actually met the Prince several times before. The first occasion was in the South of France when I was staying there with John Lyle. We saw this man on a bike cycling towards us and when he went past I said: "That's Prince Philip!" He turned round and waved and I curtsied. More recently I attended a ball at the In and Out club in London with Jamie. Jamie introduced me and Prince Philip said: "Ahh, I know Headcorn… Lashenden." He obviously remembered it from the war, having been on active service, which was rather rewarding. I had also been to another garden party at Buckingham Palace with Chris, in connection with his regiment.

I was on the selection committee for prospective Conservative parliamentary candidates for Hastings – I was really nasty! I used to delve into people's CVs more than other members would. In those days the offices were up three flights of stairs in an old building on the seafront. The roof leaked and one night during a meeting there was a huge gale blowing and we all sat waiting for the beautiful but somewhat rickety old windows to blow in!

When Jacqui Lait was running for parliament I canvassed for her. I was extremely quick and energetic and managed to cover a lot of ground. I never went in to drink tea with anyone as some did, I just rushed around encouraging people to vote for us. I got on well with Jacqui and spent time talking to her mother who was interested in race horses, as I was. After Jacqui lost her seat we were both very active in endeavouring to get Mark Coote elected.

I was also on the branch social committee and did a great deal of fundraising for the local party. I hosted all kinds of events at No 5 and also in the garden of Marigold. Sometimes I held coffee mornings, but often organised lunches and cheese and wine parties and Robin and I would shoot off to France beforehand to stock up on wine, cheese and pate and serve it all with our own homemade pickles. We would usually invite a speaker, such as the local MP. We have had up to 100 people at No 5, despite its small proportions. We would "gut" the cottage and put all we could into the garage and then erect tented gazebos in the garden. We used to raise impressive amounts of money with these gatherings; once we managed to collect £900.

We always held the Aldeburgh golf match suppers at No 5 – that meant 26 people for a four-course, sit-down meal! We used the huge table from The Firs and then added on card tables to accommodate everyone else. I didn't have a dishwasher in those days but Robin was very good at helping and did the washing-up!

Robin and I played an active part in village life. We belonged to the tennis club in Pett – in earlier days I had partnered Ronnie Watson and Dilys Cooke there and we won virtually everything – and continued to be involved in the Preservation Trust and the Residents' Association. Elizabeth had been a founder member of the Pett Level Rescue Boat.

I still rode as often as possible and, some years before, had been fortunate enough to meet the racehorse trainer Henry Candy through Gordon and Jean Farrer. Henry was a friend of Mary Kent who owned Telham Place at Battle. She was a real enthusiast, as was her black maid and cook, a very lively and engaging character, who would look up the races and then we would all discuss racing together, sitting round the kitchen table. Henry used to come down to visit Mary. He was very dashing and I got to know him and his parents, Derek and Cherry, quite well. He invited me up to Wantage in Oxfordshire to ride out and exercise his horses on the gallops, which was a huge privilege and an extremely thrilling experience.

Living right on the sea's doorstep as we do, flooding was always a possibility, but I never let it bother me. In really wild weather I used to soak old pillows and pile them up in front of the door; they are just as effective as sandbags, if not more so. I still keep some old pillows handy but, in latter years, I had a soakaway drain put into the garden and the step built up. The sea did come into the old conservatory on one occasion and then later the garden flooded – it looked just like a swimming pool but Jamie brought down his fire-fighting pump from Headcorn and sorted it out. Matters did improve after the sea wall was extended and the old groynes were replaced.

For many years I would swim every day, winter and summer, and became known as "the mad woman by the sea"! I tried a wetsuit but I couldn't get the damn thing on or off. I lost my temper with it; it was impossible! It was only when I started having problems with my knees and hips that I stopped, but I still go in when the weather is warm and the sea more inviting.

The sea wall runs directly past the back of the cottages and it's quite amusing to hear people's comments as they wander past: "They're ever so nice but they're all 'oliday 'omes"; "I wouldn't want to live there; bet the sea comes over"; "Ooh, they're ever so small" ; "Ooh, they're 'aving a *party*; look at all that wine."

When Rosie was in the garden at Marigold, it would be: "There's an 'orse in there!" After Robin started a wildflower meadow in Marigold it was: "Ooh look, they haven't cut their grass." I'm tempted to leave a tape recorder at the end of the garden. People seem to think you can't hear! I actually took issue with one couple who caught me on a bad day and, in my most superior voice, told them: "It's *not* a holiday home, we *live* here and it's *not* small, we have *three* bedrooms!" (We did, in those days; now we have just one large one.)

As we now lived quite near to Headcorn Robin and I saw Chris quite frequently. The two men had a lot in common, particularly their Army backgrounds, and got on well. One winter Robin and I planned to go skiing with Jamie. Robin's attempts to try the sport before had always come to grief for one reason or another but Jamie, a real enthusiast and excellent skier, was determined to get him on to the slopes. He was very athletic and played hockey for Teddington and Ipswich and cricket for West Norfolk so we all thought he would enjoy being on skis as we did.

We spent the night before our planned trip at Headcorn so we would be ready to go off in the morning but, during the night, there was a very heavy snowfall, so heavy that the roof of the hangar that Chris had built to house extra planes collapsed on to the aircraft inside. It was a real disaster and Chris was insistent that it was "all hands on deck", so our trip was cancelled. Two of the 12 planes housed in the hangar were badly damaged. Chris appealed to the Royal Engineers who used to train on the farm and had built a bridge over the River Beult which flowed through the fields. Assisted by Chris, Jamie and Robin, the men strove to sort out all the chaos. I helped, too, and also did lots of cooking and fed them all. Poor Robin never did get to ski!

Although our relations with Chris were cordial it didn't stop him dealing me the cruellest of blows on an occasion when he was really angry with me. He could be cantankerous and irascible – I was used to that – and we often argued over Jamie as I felt he was overworking him. But one particular row ended in a personal tragedy for me.

I still had some of my possessions – many of them extremely precious photographs and other mementoes of my early life and Jamie and Elizabeth's childhoods – stored in an attic room at Headcorn where there was plenty of space. Robin had some books and other items there, too. Chris was happy with this arrangement. But when Jamie was about 28 or 29 their relationship went through a stormy stage. Chris wouldn't buy Jamie a car and was extremely annoyed when I made him buy an old Volvo shooting brake.

Jamie took the car to France as he had a girlfriend over there, but it broke down. He called me and I went over on a commercial flight with bag loads of spares and helped him repair it. Chris was incandescent about the incident, especially when I refused to tell him where Jamie was; I didn't think it was wise.

My former husband certainly reaped his revenge. He backed a trailer up to the farmhouse door, got all my precious belongings from the attic room, and had farm staff take them away and burn them. Irreplaceable pictures of my childhood, schooldays, of people I loved, of me as a debutante, photographs of the children, our happy holidays, things they had made, treasured gifts – all were gone. Robin also lost some of his children's treasured books, photographs and possessions, too as well as photographs of his days at Winchester and in the army.

When I found out I was hysterical. I was screaming: "Where are they? Where are they?" I didn't understand how someone who had once loved me and whom I still considered a good friend could have carried out such a hateful and destructive act. For months afterwards I had nightmares about it. I was utterly distraught. For some reason, though, Chris didn't destroy my wedding dress.

However, despite his cruel behaviour, I helped out when Chris became ill and Jamie was on holiday. He had a new hip but it became infected. He was on crutches, which he called his "pogo sticks", and still managed to drive his old Rover, exercise his dogs on the runway at Headcorn and do the RT transmission at the airfield, but he gradually deteriorated. He wouldn't take his pills properly and refused to use an exercise bicycle that we got for him to strengthen his muscles.

I used to nurse him and stayed at Headcorn to cook and look after him if Jamie was away but he would often say: "Oh, stop fussing." Eventually he had to go into a nursing home and he died there, in 1999. A memorial service was held in a hangar at Headcorn and it was absolutely crowded, so many people wanted to attend. The police were on hand to direct all the traffic. Jamie and Elizabeth flew low over the airfield in a Cessna 172 as a tribute to Chris, and they both scattered their father's ashes over the runway from the plane. It was a very moving day.

The best thing about moving back to Sussex was, of course, that I was nearer to Jamie and his family and was more than happy to help out with my grandchildren. In 1994 Jamie had married his girlfriend Valerie, who is the most marvellous vet and has her surgery on the edge of the aerodrome at Headcorn. They made their home at The White House, where Jamie continued to live after Chris's death, and eventually had two daughters, Alice and Emily, whom I adore and who I hope adore me! When they were small they went to nursery schools in Headcorn and Pluckley. The schools, quite rightly, were very careful about who picked the children up at the end of the day but the girls always flew into my arms. I was so proud (and still am).

When the girls were older they went to Saint Ronan's School in Hawkhurst; the 3,500 acre Tongwood estate had previously been owned by Charles Gunther, who had made his fortune as chairman of the parent company of Oxo, and he added on to the house. I would pick the girls up from there nearly every Friday and take them back home, where I would feed and bath them and read them endless stories – there were always pleas for "one more, Grandma"! They were very happy at Saint Ronan's and encouraged to excel in work, music and games. The girls then both passed the very demanding and highly competitive entrance exam to Cranbrook School – Emily came sixth out of 100 – where they are thriving.

The girls are both superb at sport, are brilliant skiers and swim like fishes. They also play netball, tennis, hockey and rounders. Ponies and riding are a major part of their lives – like they were in mine. They had a Shetland called Echo to start with – very strong and naughty, but adorable. Val taught them to ride and Nicky Hardwick, whom I taught and who is the daughter of my old doctor at Headcorn, gives them specialist coaching. They have two beautiful ponies, 14.2 hands, and win nearly everything they go in for – they have no fear and will jump anything! Although they are bigger and more independent these days, seeing them when they have the time is one of my greatest pleasures.

Robin's sons all have lovely families now, too – he has 16 grandchildren and two great-granddaughters. Matthew, William and Luke live in East Anglia and Simon lives in Aberdeen. We see them as often as we can and recently drove up to Aberdeen to spend time with Simon and his family. He is a keen environmentalist and works as a trouble-shooter in that field for BP. He cycles 15 miles to work and back, rather than driving, whenever the weather allows it. His lovely Scottish farmhouse has four woodstoves and he has huge tree trunks delivered to feed them, which he delights in chain-sawing and chopping up himself. He has the biggest log pile Robin and I have ever seen!

Matthew is chief executive of the Mayor's Fund for London, which works with disadvantaged children and young people. He's brilliant at sports, anything to do with a stick and a ball, and likes cricket, golf and tennis. In fact, his whole family takes after him and his wife, Lucy, an excellent golfer and good at all sports.

William is a management consultant to the NHS and also Rear Commodore of the Royal Harwich Yacht Club. He has always sailed competitively and the classic boat he now races, an Excalibur 36, is his pride and joy.

Luke, the youngest, is a very successful magazine publisher and has proved himself extremely talented at building up businesses. He is a member of Rye golf club, while Will and Matthew belong to Aldeburgh and Simon plays in Scotland. From time to time the boys come down and play with Robin at Rye, which is great fun for all of us.

I feel extremely fortunate that Robin and I both have such lovely families and that we all get on so well.

Pett Level as it used to be, safe enough for sheep to graze along the roadside

I was extremely proud when Robin was made Chairman of Rother District Council.
Scrabble and Scrumpy had to get in on the act, of course!

Life at Pett Level included wonderful canters along the sand on my beloved Rosie

The Day I Nearly Died

Some years before Chris died, I suffered the most horrendous accident and was extremely fortunate to survive. One afternoon, as it was getting dusk, I went along to the field to call Rosie in. "Come on darling, I've got a lovely supper for you," I said to her, and slipped some bailer twine round her neck to lead her into the stable. Another horse had recently joined her in the field and suddenly it turned round and, for absolutely no reason, lashed out furiously with both hind legs, hammering its hooves into my side and stomach – it gave me "both barrels", as we call it. I lost consciousness. When I eventually came round I could only see brown and I thought: "I'm dead", and passed out again. This happened twice and then I realised that my beloved Rosie was standing over me, to protect me, and it was her brown tummy that I had seen.

I knew if I was to have any hope of surviving I had to summon help and, although I was in agony and the most profound distress, I decided to try to crawl along the rough, unmade track to the home of my good friend, Lorna Hogan, who lived just two houses away from the field and looked after Rosie when we were away. When I slithered towards the gate the most amazing thing happened, and it is something I will never forget; it seemed like a miracle to me. Rosie placed herself above me, again to protect me, and walked gently forward as I struggled on my hands and knees towards the gate. Somehow I managed to open and shut the gate and dragged myself to Lorna's door. There, astonishingly, another animal came to my aid. Lorna's dog never barked when I appeared as it knew me but, on this occasion, it did – and Lorna found me collapsed on her step.

Lorna was utterly calm and efficient, as she always is, and immediately called an ambulance but when the ambulance men arrived my First Aid knowledge came back to me and I told them to be extremely careful how they moved me. Because of my medical experience I knew I was very badly injured and had internal bleeding – I didn't realise, though, quite how serious it was. I asked them to fetch a chair from the ambulance for me and just leave me to do my own thing. I was taken to the Royal East Sussex Hospital in Hastings. The attack had been so violent that I had the imprints of the horse's hooves on my skin. It was discovered that all the ribs on my left side were broken and that one had pierced a lung; my spleen was also ruptured. I could hardly breathe. The doctors told me they were going to operate immediately – but they warned me that there wasn't much chance of survival. I was screaming for morphine I was in such pain.

I was given a splenectomy and the surgeons attempted to fish bits of broken rib out of my body; they couldn't mend the broken ones and didn't know if my damaged lung, which they had patched, would work again. After the operation my lung filled with fluid and I couldn't breathe; I was in agony. My lung had to be drained and it was the most horrible, painful procedure involving three nurses, who were there mainly to hold me down. The doctor inserted a needle into my back and 1.5 litres of fluid were extracted. When I had to have it done a second time I begged for sedation, or at least to be put in the kind of frame that we had used for similar procedures when I was working in the hospital in Canada, but I was told it wasn't possible.

Meanwhile, Lorna continued to be amazing. She left messages for Robin, who wasn't at home. When he did arrive, Richard Allen, a colleague of his from the golf club, who was in charge of the A&E department when I was admitted, gave him the grim diagnosis. Jamie was summoned and drove like hell, appearing at my bedside still dressed in his overalls. Elizabeth subsequently flew back from America.

I was in terrible pain. When I needed X-rays I was wheeled miles down the bumpy old corridors of the RESH to the department. I screamed every time my bed on wheels hit a hump and nearly passed out. However, despite the doctors' gloomy predictions, I did gradually recover – they said it was because I was so fit, but I also spent a fortune on special pain-killing injections that were done privately. Sometimes, if I drove myself to the clinic, I had to sit in the car for ages afterwards, weeping, until I found the strength to drive myself home. It took me a year to get over the trauma of it all. Eventually, though, my ribs rejoined but my left lung still doesn't function properly and, with no spleen, I have no immune system, so I have to be extremely vigilant about my health and take great care to avoid germs and colds and flu. Pneumonia could be fatal for me.

People were so kind while I was in hospital. I received so many cards and flowers that it was hardly possible to get into my room – I wrote hundreds of thank-you letters. Members of the Guinea Pig Club, the Battle of Britain pilots whose terribly burnt faces were reconstructed by the brilliant surgeon Archibald McIndoe, of which I was an enthusiastic long-term supporter and fund-raiser, came to see me and brought me a huge bouquet.

During this time Robin looked after the heroic Rosie for me. He adored her, nicknaming her "Petal", and marvelled at how easy she was. She would pee in a bucket so we rarely had wet bedding to contend with. I could always do anything with her; she was more like a dog and seemed to understand everything I said to her. However, the accident left me very nervous of horses and I thought I would never be able to ride again. When I went on holiday to Djerba with Jean Farrer, poor skinny Arab horses were galloped along the beach and Jean put herself between them and me as I was trembling so much. However, a year after my accident, in some trepidation, I got back up on Rosie and it was as if I had never been away. She responded to me just as gently and lovingly and as loyally as ever. We progressed, very slowly, out of the gate at Marigold and along on to the grass verge. I then rather hesitantly tried a trot and, amazingly, it was all perfect again, just as if I had ridden her only yesterday, not with a whole year's gap in between.

Rosie was a unique horse, one in a million and everyone loved her. She was her own person: if people said they couldn't ride she would plod gently along with them on her back. If they said they could, and it turned out they couldn't, she would shrug them gently off over the side! Thankfully, we had a few more years of companionship before she tragically got cast – which is when a horse can't get up. This happened three times – I managed to get her back on to her feet but on one occasion she injured herself when she banged her head. She also developed arthritis and our blacksmith, Jon Martlew, who became a real friend, had trouble lifting her legs to shoe her.

Eventually I was forced to face the fact that Rosie's days were coming to an end and she would have to be put down. Robin took her to Headcorn – poor Robin; I was in no fit state. My daughter-in-law, Val, put her to sleep at her practice on the farm at Headcorn and Rosie was buried there. She was 32. It was one of the saddest days of my life. I could never love another horse as much as I loved Rosie and I will never forget her, she brought me such happiness and love.

*About to set off with Jamie and my grandaughters Emily, left, and Alice,
for an adventure in a Rapide*

Everything's Up in the Air

Just as I had been proved wrong when I lay in my hospital bed imagining that I would never be able to ride again, I turned out to be equally mistaken in my assumption that I would never be able to return to my other great passion… flying.

With all the diversions during my years in Suffolk I had let my flying slip. I did a little at Swanton Morley and also at Ipswich for fun but it had become very expensive and I began to feel "been there, done that", so my licence lapsed and I got involved in other things. I really didn't expect to fly seriously again. When we moved back to Pett Level I would go up with Jamie from time to time. He had a Cherokee Warrior and we would occasionally fly Alice and Emily to visit his parents-in-law in Cheltenham. Jamie would do the RT and I would take the controls.

Elizabeth gained her aviation licence in the States. When I visit her in America we often go flying together and we have had some adventures. On one occasion we were flying from Orange County to Catalina Island, off California. We radioed ahead to the airstrip seeking permission to land. The controller put us on hold and we had to fly round and round. We again asked to "join the finals". He replied: "Negative." There were no other aircraft in the vicinity and when I asked why we were on hold he said he had liked listening to our voices on the radio!

In the end, we didn't find this very amusing. It's challenging enough landing there as it is, because it's a mountainous area and if you don't stop quickly enough once you touch down you shoot off the end of the runway into the sea! Also, the longer we were kept up in the air the more the hiring fee for the aircraft mounted. When we told the people at Torrance Airport what had happened they said there had been a few "problems" with air control staff on Catalina.

We usually fly out of Torrance Airport, or Zamperini Field, in California with Reza Birjandi from Pacific Skies who is endlessly kind and supportive. It's a friendly airfield and has a great history which I find fascinating. It came into being after the attack on Pearl Harbor when existing airports were commandeered and new ones quickly constructed. Torrance, then known as the Lomita Flight Strip, was one of these.

The airport then sent off four squadrons of P-38 fighters to join the war and many of the pilots distinguished themselves. When the war ended Torrance temporarily housed Japanese Americans who had been interned in Europe.

In 2012 I took up a Cessna, which I liked, and a Cirrus, which is extremely fast but which I didn't warm to – the trim is very awkward in your hand. I flew miles down the coast and over LA airport – imagine being allowed to do that over Heathrow!

There are a lot of planes trailing banners and signwriting in the skies in that area and I wanted to dodge them. I suggested to the PI that I drop 100 feet and, although he was surprised, he agreed so I did so and flew under the other planes that were in the way. We had planned to land at Palm Springs but it was too hot – the intense heat affects the time it takes to get off the ground, so I was rather disappointed. But we flew on to San Diego and as I got plenty of flying in and did several turns and other manoeuvres, that made up for it.

In 2013 I spent several weeks with Elizabeth having medical treatment from her amazing healing hands and a top-to-toe MOT she kindly arranged for me. I visited my stepmother Helen and several old friends but my lovely daughter and I still found time to go flying. Elizabeth hired a Cessna 172 and we flew out of John Wayne airport which is vast with jets landing and taking off every few minutes.

Elizabeth had told the instructor that I knew how to fly but he was obviously pretty nervous about being flown by a lady in her 80th year, however experienced. As we got up speed I said I thought there was something wrong with the ailerons as I was getting resistance. "Well, I've got my feet on the rudder pedals, too!" he said.

I wanted to look at a wartime airport and as we flew near it the ATC put us on hold and we had to do 360s, ie fly round in circles. We were flying into the sun and the instructor said he would do the manoeuvres if I wanted him to. I said I was quite happy and would prefer to do them. I said I would do them on the instruments and be "in the office" and Elizabeth would keep an eye out for other planes.

I did four 360s and thoroughly enjoyed it. I didn't lose any height at all which is quite commendable and eventually the instructor began to relax a little. I think he realised I could actually fly and wasn't going to put him into the nearest mountain!

I eventually landed the Cessna safely back at John Wayne which, with the air traffic coming and going, takes a bit of careful negotiation.

During a trip to New Zealand and Australia I grasped some opportunities to fly. I spent two weeks in New Zealand visiting the North and South Islands and went up in a seaplane, a Cessna 180, and the pilot let me take the controls for a while. In Australia, I visited my cousin, Philip, an orthopaedic surgeon. I went gliding with one of his friends: we had a tug launch and stayed up for 25 minutes. I had the controls in flight and followed through with the landings – it was all very thrilling!

My flying has certainly been diverse. I had a holiday in Africa with Jean Irvine Robertson, whose brother-in-law, George Irvine Robertson, was head of Nairobi Hospital. He had a house in Mombasa and we flew on from Nairobi for a visit. They had an old VW car which tended to break down, so we soon found it was advisable always to keep £5 handy in currency to bribe the police.

One day we were going to a special restaurant but it was situated down a very bumpy track in a somewhat hostile environment. The car, of course, broke down at a lonely spot and I had to repair it with one eye looking over my shoulder the whole time.

I met a vet out there who flew everywhere because of the distances involved in his work and he invited me to go on a call with him. Flying is certainly the way to see Africa and all the game – it was amazing. We spotted pink flamingos on one of the vast lakes, but it was drying up and the vet was extremely concerned about it.

The vet needed spares for his Cessna 172 and I was pleased to be able to help him by shipping some out on my return, as Chris had the necessary contacts to provide them.

We also saw a sick turtle just along from the house. It was a fascinating creature but, sadly, I believe it died; the local people didn't seem to treat animals very well.

Jean and I went on to the Treetops Hotel in Kenya where the Queen learnt that her father had died and she was to accede to the throne. It was pretty primitive and I was disappointed that the gallery from where you viewed all the animals drinking at the lake was protected by glass, so it was difficult to take really sharp photographs through it. We stayed in little rooms in Treetops with the loo quite a long way down the passage and although the food was "different", we managed not to get ill.

I have one particularly touching memory from that visit. There was a doctor whose wife was in a wheelchair – she had wanted to visit Treetops before she died. Her husband asked me if I would kindly look after her "for the ladies' side of things', ie taking her to the lavatory, and, of course, I was delighted to help.

Aviation has brought me into contact with so many amazing characters. I recently bumped into Charlie Brown, who flies a Spitfire from Lydd, giving people the chance to appreciate this wonderful aircraft from another plane flying alongside. He recognised me and we talked over old times.

On one occasion at Lydd I took over the controls of a Calidus gyrocopter belonging to my friend Andrea. She flew in with her instructor and he took me up and we had a very instructive and exciting time – I loved every minute.

When I look back now at all my years of flying I'm very pleased I did it all when I did. I was lucky to have such a good instructor as George Moorwood in Canada and so much help and support from Neville Browning, and fortunate to be able to have two planes of my own. In those days I was quite unusual, which is why the press were so interested. There had been female pilots, such as Amy Johnson and Harriet Quimby, but not so many others, so I suppose a "flying mum" or "flying farmer's wife" was newsworthy. Now all kinds of women fly and it's not so remarkable. When people see pieces about me in the local press today, they say: "We never knew you *flew*," but you don't go about saying: "I'm a pilot!", do you?

I am currently the regional ambassador for the South-East of England branch of the British Women Pilots' Association, based at Headcorn, and we hold regular meetings, sometimes at my cottage. In 2012 we celebrated the 100th anniversary of Harriet Quimby's flight across the English Channel – the first woman to do so. We had a fly-out to Le Touquet which, despite the challenging weather, was quite an occasion. I was first a member of the BWPA, which was formed to encourage women to become involved in aviation, in 1963. Lettice Curtis, who flew bombers during the war and went on to have a distinguished career in the aviation industry, was involved in our branch and we would take women who didn't fly over to France to give them a taste of what it was like. I'm delighted to be back in the association now, working for the new branch at Headcorn Aerodrome, with the help of Jamie.

Although I no longer have a licence, and some might feel that my age is against me, I must confess that I have been bitten by the flying bug of late and can't help wondering if I should take to the air again in a more serious way.

Flying has become increasingly complicated over the years – on the RT you're talking to someone all the time – and also much more expensive. I'm not sure I'd be able to pass the exams today – they include RT, air law, navigation and meteorology, but I have flown a Robin and a Cessna at Headcorn with various instructors and thoroughly enjoyed it all.

One instructor was reluctant to allow me to taxi the plane back to its site because of all the ruts in the ground caused by the rain but I know the techniques for doing that very well and insisted on doing it myself – after all, I've been doing it for ever and used to taxi my own plane straight into its hangar! Another instructor, Gavin, thought there was no reason why I shouldn't get a licence again. He suggested an NPPL, which allows you to fly in England but not abroad.

Robin and Jamie have been hugely encouraging and so have my granddaughters – "*Do* it, Grandma!" – but I'm currently considering the options.

I'd need to swat up on the things: such as take-off, cross-wind, down-wind, base and finals. It used to be BUMF – base, undercarriage, mixture, fuel and flap – but they've changed it to eight letters and I need to clarify all that. But I'm always checking everything anyway, as I'm very instrument-oriented and so safety conscious.

At the moment, it's just wonderful to be flying again and I'm so happy to be a pilot at 80! I'm not allowed to take anyone up with me as I don't have my licence but I can still do greasers and my lovely GP, Doctor Chopra, pronounced me fit to fly after a recent comprehensive medical and said I am really good for my age. So who knows where it all might lead? The sky really is the limit!

*The original Women Pilots'
Association badge
from 1963*

*A report of an early meeting
of the Headcorn branch
of the WPA and a shot of me
with other members*

Headcorn Ladies' Evening (Sat 21 April)

I was recently invited by a newly-rejoined BWPA member, Di Patten, to speak to a group of women pilots flying from Headcorn Aerodrome (EGKH) in Kent. Di (with her first husband Christopher Freeman) started developing Headcorn in the 1960s to become the active airfield it is today. Her son Jamie Freeman is the current owner/manager.

The brief was to engage with as many local women pilots as possible with a view to establishing a BWPA South East regional group based at Headcorn. The ladies here are already a very active as a group and Jamie felt that becoming part of a larger organisation would help to encourage more women into aviation.

Around 25 people turned out for the event and we were treated to a short slide show by Di covering some of her many and varied aviation adventures in addition to my talk on the BWPA and a very tasty chilli con carne!

We have gained a number of new members as a result of the evening and I am confident that the Headcorn group will be great role models to encourage more women into aviation.

Caroline Gough-Cooper

6

*The Cirrus's control panel showing how I dropped 100 feet to dodge
other planes trailing banners above the Californian coast;
my P1 was rather surprised!*

Sailing in the States – my daughter Elizabeth takes the helm...

...then it was my turn

*Mission accomplished – just after touching down in the
Cirrus at Torrance Airport in California*

An affectionate moment on the airstrip with my wonderful daughter

With Reza who accompanied me when we flew out of Torrance Airport

A helicopter trip to the Grand Canyon was a highlight of one of my trips to the USA

FLIGHT CERTIFICATE

0418 713 903

gliding.caboolture.org.au

Caboolture Gliding Club Inc certifies that

DIANA PATTEN

today experienced the exhilaration of silent flight in glider VH- COC of type IS28

Pilot PETER STEPHENSON Date 28-5-2010

Gliding while on holiday in Australia was wonderful

I flew this Cessna when I was in New Zealand

After we landed, I was privileged to be allowed a peek at the controls of the 747 in which I flew home from New Zealand

Of course I had to try a helicopter – with James Tuke, MD of Thurston Helicopters which is based at Headcorn...

...and my friend Andrea's Calidus gyrocopter – at Lydd, 2012

...just to prove I did it!

Pre flight checks at Headcorn, summer 2014

*It was touching that so many Guinea Pigs attended the memorial service
for my former husband Chris, who had raised a lot of money
for them during his lifetime.
The hangar at Headcorn, where the service was held, was packed*

The Guinea Pigs

My glamorous aunt, Paddy Naismith, first got me involved with Archibald McIndoe's famous "Guinea Pigs". The brilliant surgeon pioneered facial reconstruction on the Battle of Britain pilots who were horrifically burnt during the war. Their Hurricanes and Spitfires had powerful engines that ran on aviation fuel, which was highly inflammable – if a plane was hit by enemy fire and caught alight the pilots often suffered terrible injuries. Some of McIndoe's "boys" endured more than 30 operations. The worst problem for the surgeon was the rejection of skin grafts and his patients were called Guinea Pigs as he honed his amazing skills through experience.

Because of their disfigurement the Guinea Pigs sometimes found it hard to integrate into society but McIndoe went to great lengths to ensure they were accepted and Aunt Paddy and others like her were instrumental in this. She knew Archibald through her flying and was fond of him and his wife, Connie. She was keen on voluntary work and offered to help – she could bluff her way into anything! I first met the Guinea Pigs in my teens and I knew that if I showed a flicker of hesitation because of their looks I would be subjected to one of my aunt's ominous glares.

Paddy was my father's sister. The Naismiths were creative and arty and the family also comprised my aunts Sheila, a designer and artist; Gilly, Elizabeth and Julie. Elizabeth was married to Paddy Quirk, an architect and structural engineer who famously designed folding doors as a room divider. They had a beautiful Rolls. One of my ancestors, James Naismith, was quite a well-known artist. My grandmother, who was an Irish Redmond and brought the red hair, which Paddy, Gilly and I inherited, into the family, was also an accomplished artist.

My aunt was an extremely lively figure who also raced cars. In the Thirties Barbara Cartland, a "Brooklands Babe", decided to stage a race at the famous track to help to answer a question posed by Harold Pemberton, motoring correspondent of the Daily Express, who asked whether women could drive cars with as much skill as men. First across the line, according to Pemberton, was Paddy Naismith, but other reports claim she came third. As well as being a pilot, Aunt Paddy was an actress. Her red hair got her noticed and Logie Baird used her striking image in his early experiments with television.

Paddy would take coach parties of the Guinea Pigs to the theatre in London and usually managed to secure free tickets and meals for them at hotels. The "boys" loved their beer and if the pubs weren't open Paddy would knock on their doors and ask them to open up, saying: "I have very important people on my bus!"

We helped to organise fundraising events to mark the club's anniversarys at the Felbridge Hotel in East Grinstead and we were also involved with a big open day at the local Queen Victoria Hospital, where the operations were done, so that people could come in and see how everything worked. I also helped with a golf day at Birch Grove, Harold Macmillan's former home. The course was built round a beautiful mansion and is exquisitely groomed and prepared. Then it was privately owned by the Chinese tycoon Larry Yung, who allowed one charity event a year on the course, provided that more than £5,000 could be raised. We provided refreshments at the ninth hole and used the manager's house to lay out a superb lunch. One of the surgeons made a speech and we raised a lot of money. I remember that it was one of the last events that Connie managed to attend.

Chris and I organised fund-raising events at Headcorn, including an air show. The Guinea Pigs were given a special tour of the museum and Chris took those who wanted to fly up for bumps and circuits.

I also took part in a long-distance sponsored ride round the South of England and raised about £3,000. Daddy was very proud of me taking part and sponsored me for £500. It was great fun. Jamie came to wave me off but he was late so arrived in a helicopter. Aunt Julie came, too, and we were all on the front of the Guinea Pig magazine. Robin was my back-up and various friends mucked in as grooms. The Grand National winner Aldaniti led a parade through East Grinstead to start us off and I rode behind on Rosie. We went right through the town and the traffic was halted. The ride was mostly on private land through the most beautiful estates that one never usually gets a chance to see, except from the air. We stopped to eat and to sleep in pubs. I did two days: I went as far as Eastbourne and covered more than 60 miles.

I got to know some of the Guinea Pigs extremely well. Jack Alloway was one who became a friend. When I did my charity ride on Rosie he insisted I had to be properly dressed and sent me his Guinea Pig tie. I wore it proudly with my shirt and still treasure it.

A significant number of Guinea Pigs were Canadians and they would fly in for some fund-raising events. Arthur Askey did a very successful cabaret at the Felbridge and I was given a photograph of him singing his "Busy Bee" song with the "boys" round him at the piano. I was also presented with a special scroll to commemorate the Guinea Pig Club's 50th anniversary. They were often great characters and their damaged faces didn't seem to stop them being a hit with the ladies, I seem to recall! One, named Tubby, always made a point of jumping into the pool at the Felbridge with all his clothes on – and sometimes without!

I have greatly enjoyed my fund-raising and the GPC has been kind enough to recognise my efforts. At a recent lunch I went to with Robin, the social secretary, Jack Perry, said he had a surprise for someone – it was me. I was presented with a Guinea Pig badge – it was a great honour and I was absolutely delighted. I went to another lunch with Jamie after there had been a play about the club put on in the Midlands. We had been unable to attend, but the actors and actresses were sitting at the tables with us all.

I noticed on the list of speeches that I was to give the vote of thanks – I hadn't prepared anything and could hardly eat my meal! I managed to scribble down a few notes and recalled the sponsored ride and Aldaniti. Fortunately I did have something up my sleeve because Jack Perry's wife, Mary Lou, had done a huge amount of work for the charity, too, and I had brought along a Pooley's bear from Headcorn to give to her, so at least I was able to end my speech with a flourish!

I was recently delighted to be invited to meet the Princess Royal when she unveiled the new McIndoe Memorial Statue at East Grinstead. As you can see from the photograph of the occasion, on page 135, we had a very amusing conversation about flying and riding! I have had some wonderful times raising money for the GPC and met some amazing, inspiring characters. As a pilot myself, as well as a grateful and unscathed survivor of the war, I feel I really couldn't have chosen a more rewarding and worthwhile cause to support.

I am sometimes asked to give talks on flying and I am happy to donate any fees that I receive to the Blond McIndoe Research Foundation which now carries out research into treating burns and similar traumatic injuries.

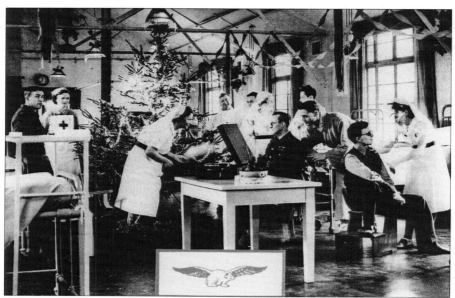

A ward at the Queen Victoria Hospital in East Grinstead
where the Guinea Pigs were treated

Archibald McIndoe, the eminent plastic surgeon, entertains some of his Guinea Pigs

THE GUINEA PIG CLUB'S

25th ANNIVERSARY
"EVE OF DINNER" DANCE

FRIDAY, 23rd SEPTEMBER

AT YE OLDE FELBRIDGE HOTEL

Dancing to the Music of
Peter Ricardo and his Band
FROM 9.00 P.M.—2.00 A.M.

ALL STAR CABARET - TOMBOLA STALL

TICKETS 25/- *including Buffet*

Fun and fund-raising on behalf of the Guinea Pigs

*Ready for the off on my two-day fund-raising ride on Rosie.
From left my friend and supporter Adele, Aunt Julie and Jamie
with some Guinea Pigs who came to see me off*

Mrs Diana Patten

Blond McIndoe Research Foundation
Charity Number: 1106240

EGBA · EAST GRINSTEAD BUSINESS ASSOCIATION

working in collaboration

 EAST GRINSTEAD TOWN COUNCIL

Mr. Baljit Dheansa, Chairman of Blond McIndoe Research Foundation

requests the pleasure of your company

to celebrate the unveiling of the McIndoe Memorial Statue

by

HRH The Princess Royal

Monday, 9th June 2014

RSVP
jacquie.pinney@blondmcindoe.org
Tel: 01342 414052

11am to 3pm
Dress code: Lounge Suit/Day Dress

This celebratory Guinea Pig scroll is one of my treasures

*I so enjoyed meeting the Princess Royal at the unveiling of the beautiful
McIndoe Memorial Statue at East Grinstead – not least because
it gave me the opportunity to wear a hat!*

TELEVISION IN COLOUR

J. L. BAIRD'S NEW ADVANCE

While the theory of television was well-known long before 1926, no practical success had been achieved in transmitting television images. It had only been possible to send shadows of shapes; in other words, the televised image was then nothing more than a transmitted shadowgraph. On January 27th, 1926, however, for the first time, true living pictures—that is, images modelled by light and shade—were shown by a system of television invented by John Logie Baird, a demonstration being given to members of the Royal Institution and other scientists on that date. This achievement created a sensation which most of us remember, and much appeared in the Press at that time, a good deal of it greatly exaggerated. What was actually shown in that year is simply and authoritatively described in an article by Dr. Alexander Russell, F.R.S. a past president of the I.E.E. and of the Physical Society, writing in "Nature" of 3rd July, 1926. He states :—

"We saw the transmission by television of living human faces, the proper

The first photograph of a television image ever published, the image on the screen of Mr. Baird's first televisor in 1926

(Miss Paddy Naismith, the well-known Airwoman)
The first photograph of a colour television image ever published, the image on the screen of Mr. Baird's 600 line colour televisor.

My aunt's Paddy's stunning colouring made her a perfect choice
for the first television image ever published. An actress and pilot, she introduced me to the
Guinea Pigs and worked extremely hard on their behalf

My paternal grandmother, nee Redmond,
gave Aunt Paddy and me our distinctive red hair

Aunt Paddy in her days as an air hostess, beside the iconic Junker 55,
three-engined plane – it had one on each wing and another on the nose.
It was 60 feet long and had a 96 foot wingspan

An iconic shot of my glamorous aunt, by Bassano Ltd, May 7, 1934
National Portrait Gallery

Aunt Paddy was so stylish
— I believe she designed the windscreen wiper goggles herself

Scary Stuff

I have logged an awful lot of flying hours – it's not something I talk about – but I've only had a couple of close shaves. I think many of the accidents in small planes are due to pilot error or 'showing off'. You really need to know how to handle a plane properly so that you can correct spins and get yourself out of trouble. Some aircraft aren't suitable for certain manoeuvres such as steep turns and if you spin when you're too low you can't correct it. You just can't afford to take chances and I always insisted, and still do, that everything is perfect before I get in a plane. I have always been meticulous about my pre-flight inspections and people used to tease me about how fussy I was, but I think it's worthwhile and I'm still here, after all! My father told me never to take a plane up that I wasn't happy about and Neville Browning counselled: "Better a late Diana than the late Diana!"

However, despite my caution, Chris and I had a problem with the Auster when we were flying to the Jersey air rally one year. We were near Caen military airport in France when the engine began to splutter. Chris thought it was the plugs. I decided to land at Caen and turned off the engine so that it wouldn't be damaged in any way. Caen's two-mile runway was helpful and I landed downwind, and not into the wind, as one should. It was a perfect landing, though, and I was rather pleased with myself – but then realised that we would have to push it all the way back to the control area! I had never flown with a dead prop before so it was certainly an interesting experience.

The Auster had a Lycoming engine, which was extremely efficient but did sometimes have a problem with the plugs, as on this occasion. We had spares with us and we changed them, then I did a circuit and everything was fine so we set off again.

The controllers at Caen congratulated me on my skilled landing, which I was rather pleased about! It is said that a good landing is one you can walk away from, but I have always loved to do a perfectly smooth "greaser", which means you hardly feel a thing as you touch down. When I used to take Jamie and Elizabeth off on a trip as children they sometimes fell asleep on the way home. If I didn't wake them up when we landed they would say: "Gosh that was a greaser, *Mummy!" It was so funny.*

Another scare I had was when Chris and I had flown the Dauphin down to Dijon to be serviced. We set off for home in good weather but, south of Paris, it clamped in and the fog was impenetrable. My instruments were fine but I couldn't see anything and couldn't find a ceiling. I was trying to get through to Orly airport for some directions but couldn't make contact; it happens sometimes. Chris was map reading and said there was a small aerodrome ahead. I was down to 100 feet and decided to land there. I taxied the Dauphin in and was rather relieved to come to a stop. But the owners came rushing out and told us we had been very lucky – there were power cables nearby and we could have hit them.

Although I was quite competent and always knew I could get the Dauphin down if I needed to, I was a little unnerved by this incident. We caught the train and boat back home, leaving the Dauphin behind until the weather cleared. A couple of days later a friend flew us back to France and, as I was still shaken, we flew back side by side with the intercom going between us, which I found very reassuring.

On another occasion we were flying in Germany – I'd been at the controls for a long time and was very tired. I had my sunglasses on and was preparing to land when Chris shouted: "You're too high!"

I whipped my glasses off and realised that he was right. I had to make some hasty adjustments before we were in the right position to land – it was quite worrying and even more proof, if needed, that you can never take enough care when you're in the air.

When you have your own plane you just can't afford to risk any damage. Once, when Chris and I were intending to fly to Southend, I noticed the front oleo of the Cessna 172 W.J. we planned to take was low in hydraulic fluid and I insisted it was pumped up before we went, or we could have damaged the nose wheel when we landed. I recently landed a plane that I was flying at Headcorn because it was overheating and I thought it was dangerous. I refuse to shrug such warnings off.

Tail Piece...

Robin and I got the first of our dogs, Walter, a Yorkshire Terrier, while we were in Norfolk. Hoppy had been such a sweet companion while I was living at Headcorn that it was lovely to have another dog. We got him from Amanda Woodroffe when she was living part time at Stonewalls in Pett Level – she bred from her bitch which produced three puppies. We fell for Walter; he was such a character. We took him up to Libra, where there was no gate at the end of the drive, but Walter never went on to the road. He would ask to go out for a walk and always walked to heel. If anyone came near me he would growl; he was very protective.

When we later moved to Suffolk Walter loved the sheep and Rosie – he would ride her bareback! He went everywhere with us: in the car he rode on the parcel shelf – he loved going fast – and slept with us in our bed with Miss Guinness, our cat. She was very special, black and white – hence her name, which was initially just Guinness. Elizabeth decided we should call her Miss Guinness and after that she refused to answer to just "Guinness". She also used to jump on Rosie's back and go to sleep when the infra-red lamp was on – sometimes Rosie got fed up with her rug and preferred the lamp.

Unfortunately Miss Guinness did tend to wander across the road, to a cornfield that was good for mousing. One terrible day she was run over – Robin found her nearly dead on his way to work. The vet said there was nothing to be done but we were determined to nurse her. We turned a small antique table upside down and made a bed for her; we fed her with a pipette and gave her the injections she needed and, eventually, she began to recover. After that she was very nervous and never wandered again. When we had to move back to Pett Level she had her own little garden at the back of the cottage and was content until she died from natural causes, aged 12.

Walter sadly died at 14 and we didn't have another dog for some time, until Jamie gave me our first Jack Russell, which he and Chris had bred, for my birthday. All the Headcorn Jack Russells' names began with S so we called him Scrumpy; his mother was called Scrap. Scrumpy was a wonderful dog and looked after me very well when I later had my awful accident; he would always fetch the post from the front porch and bring it up to me. He also saved me from burglars when Robin was away on a golf tour. I was on my own in bed with Scrumpy when he suddenly shot down the stairs and out through the cat flap. I ran down in my nightie to find two big men in the back garden. Scrumpy had got one by the ankle and held on as they ran up the steps to the sea wall. I was shouting at Scrumpy and he eventually let go of the man's leg and came back to me. Apparently the men had also tried to raid the nearby Smuggler pub and the people there had alerted the police.

The officers were very kind to me and suggested I stay with the owners of the pub but I declined and said I would be fine with Scrumpy. I was all right... but in the morning I couldn't stop shaking. I phoned Jamie and he and Val came down and stayed with me all day.

The burglars were eventually caught, with the help of a farming friend of ours after they broke into his house. He followed them to Brede woods, where they were burning things in black bags. I asked the police about them later and they said that one of the men did have a nasty bite on his ankle! The word must have got around because, to this day, touch wood, we have never been burgled.

Scrumpy wasn't always angelic, though. He loved his walks but one day, when Robin was taking him along the sea wall, he went up to a man who didn't like dogs and he put his foot out. Scrumpy bit him. Robin had to arrange for his trousers to be mended and apologised profusely – fortunately the man didn't report him. Some time later Scrumpy saw the same man, who was holding an umbrella which he swiftly opened, presumably hoping for some protection! The man poked at Scrumpy with the umbrella and Scrumpy got it and chewed it to shreds. This time Robin had to give him one of his best golfing umbrellas to pacify him!

Scrumpy used to love going to the golf course and disappearing down rabbit holes but one day he went down one on the fifth hole and didn't come out. I was dreadfully worried and, leaving Robin there, I went back to the cottage to fetch a spade, hosepipe, sleeping bags and hot drinks – we weren't prepared just to leave Scrumpy down there. However, having done all that, and just as I was leaving the cottage to return to the course, fully laden, the telephone rang and it was Robin, to let me know that Scrumpy had come out again some way from where he went in. After that we trained him and his sister, Scrabble, who came to us for a short stay and never went back to Headcorn, never to go near rabbit holes or rabbits and they didn't. So don't say you can't train a Jack Russell – you can!

Sadly, Scrumpy eventually died of a heart attack in my arms on the way to the vet – but he did leave us some lovely and very amusing memories.

Scrabble and our other Jack Russell, Snoopy, lived until they were 16, having had a lovely life together. Then, sadly, they got ill within weeks of each other and, although Val did everything she could, including carrying out major surgery on them both, in the end she was unable to save them and she had to put them both to sleep. It was heart-rending but Val was marvellous and so kind – I'm lucky to have such a skilled and wonderful daughter-in-law.

Robin and I had decided not to have another pet. We planned just to enjoy having friends' dogs to stay; we thought that was the sensible option. But then we began to weaken *and Elizabeth kept saying how a puppy would be good for me… We arranged to go and see a litter of Jack Russells but the breeder let us down. Then, one day, a woman took a young, black and white Jack Russell bitch, which she had found wandering near a gipsy camp with a rope round its neck, into Val's veterinary surgery at Headcorn. The poor thing, which Val thought was about 18 months old, had obviously had pups after her first season and was very thin. She hadn't been cared for, let alone micro-chipped.*

Val called us and Robin and I went up to see her. The little dog came straight up to me… and, of course, she is now happily installed, and ruling the roost, in No 5. We have christened her Scruff and she has every conceivable comfort, from beautiful blankets to the most luxurious dog beds, all sent from America by a delighted Elizabeth!! And that puppy we were thinking about? Well, it's always possible that Scruff might need a companion…!

At the unveiling of the McIndoe Memorial Statue, June 2014

Special Thanks To

Elizabeth Freeman
Helen Naismith
Chris O'Donoghue
Robin Patten
Nick at Pixels, Rye
Robert Pooley
The Prichard Family (Jane, Robert and Sarah)
Sian Stott

About The Author

Greer Harris began her journalistic career at
the Gravesend and Dartford Reporter. She has
also worked for the Brighton Argus; the Eastern
Daily Press and Eastern Evening News and the
Daily Telegraph.